Classical - 8, 13, 17
Keynesian 9, 10, 11, 12, 13, 14

The Economics of
Uncertainty

D1323124

Central
one week loan

Please return on or before the last
date stamped below.
Charges are made for late return.

OCT 1997		11 DEC 1998
	22 MAY 1998	19 JAN 1999
30 NOV 1997		
11 NOV 1997		29 SEP 1999
		18 OCT 1999
	4 JUN 1998	
1997		
10 DEC 1997		2 OCT 1999
	13 OCT 1998	
	19 OCT 1998	6 DEC 1999
12		
DEC 1997	26 OCT 1998	11 JAN 2000
1998	2 NOV 1998	8 FEB 2000
2	12 NOV 1998	31 MAY 2000
1998		
	25 NOV 1998	
	2 DEC 1998	16 2000

The Economics of Uncertainty

C. J. McKenna

HARVESTER
WHEATSHEAF

New York   London   Toronto   Sydney   Tokyo   Singapore

First published 1986 by
Harvester Wheatsheaf
Campus 400, Maylands Avenue
Hemel Hempstead
Hertfordshire, HP2 7EZ
A division of
Simon & Schuster International Group

Typeset in 10/12pt by
Mathematical Composition Setters Ltd, Salisbury

Printed and bound in Great Britain by
Biddles Ltd, Guildford and King's Lynn

British Library Cataloguing in Publication Data

A catalogue record for this book is available from
the British Library

  ISBN 0–7450–0259–5 (hbk)
  ISBN 0–7450–0260–9 (pbk)

2 3 4 5   97 96 95 94 93

To my parents

Contents

List of Figures and Tables

Preface

In writing an 'introductory' book requiring a balance between the intuitive and the rigorous one is tempted to turn to a group of students for help. This I did, and their enthusiastic response could hardly have been anticipated. I am therefore grateful to Guy Britton, Alison Cambage, Fionnuala Earley, Pat Keating, Elliot Lewis, Mark Newnham, David Owen, Helen Parker, Helen Wilkins, Jim Wilson and Carole Young for being my first victims. At the time, they were all in the latter part of their second year at University College, Cardiff.

The idea for this book was prompted by Romesh Vaitilingam of Wheatsheaf and he has admirably maintained a tradition of that company for enthusiasm and encouragement. Sandra Simpson prepared the final typescript with great skill and efficiency.

The book is dedicated to my parents with love, and much gratitude.

Introduction

This is an introduction to economic analysis under uncertainty. A number of intermediate and advanced microeconomics texts now contain chapters and sections on aspects of uncertainty [for example, Gravelle and Rees (1981), Henderson and Quandt (1980), Laidler (1981), Layard and Walters (1978), and Varian (1978)]. However, few are able to give a full account of the basic techniques and the various applications. Some specialist books, on the other hand, while providing an invaluable guide to the breadth of the subject and its literature, do so at quite a high level of sophistication [for example Diamond and Rothschild (1978), and Hey (1979, 1981)].

This book therefore fills a gap in the range of texts available. The coverage, although not comprehensive, extends across most areas of microeconomics. The choice of topics is necessarily selective, but on the whole they are subjects which have received most attention and which are of greatest interest.

The approach adopted is to keep the analysis fairly simple. Knowledge of differential calculus, a little integration and some statistics is useful, and students who use a main microeconomics text of at least the level of Gravelle and Rees (1981) should have little difficulty with the analysis. Where possible, and appropriate, simplifying assumptions have been used and graphical expositions adopted. I have been at pains to ensure that the specific examples have contained the essence of the more general models, and where the results are stronger than may be obtained in the general case I have indicated so.

To aid the student and provide a link with existing sources each chapter is accompanied by exercises and a bibliographic guide. The exercises are not demanding and are designed largely for the reader to fill in some gaps in the text. To accompany most chapters further exercises may be found in Diamond and Rothschild (1978). The bibliographic guides do little more than point to where the interested reader should go next. Excessive referencing puts off many students, but sooner or later those who require more than a passing acquaintance with the subject must undertake a serious reading programme. Happily, there is usually a higher level and well-referenced text which may be approached before the final plunge into the original papers and primary sources. Occasionally I have referred directly to the original papers, often because the original exposition is hard to improve upon. I recommend that both the exercises and the bibliographic guides are taken seriously.

The book is suitable for use on a variety of courses at both under-graduate and postgraduate level. Primary amongst these are micro-economics and mathematical economics courses. Specialist uncertainty courses are relatively few but since the material of this book may easily be covered in one semester (North America) or in a half-course (UK) it may prompt greater exposure of this important branch of analysis to undergraduates. At the postgraduate and pro-fessional levels the book may prove useful where the reader requires a somewhat gentler introduction to uncertainty than is currently available.

The chapters follow a logical sequence, but because uncertainty economics raises new interesting questions and issues which simply do not arise under certainty the sequence is not that normally found in a standard microeconomics text.

Chapter 1 sets the scene by giving an overview of the unfamiliar territory covered by uncertainty economics. Chapters 2 and 3 explore some of the ways in which decisions may be made when the conse-quences of these decisions are not known for certain. Chapter 2 discusses several apparently reasonable rules which aid decision-making while chapter 3 provides an exposition of the most widely used tool of analysis—expected utility theory. There follow two fairly straightforward areas of application of expected utility theory. The first, in Chapter 4, looks at the theory of the firm and, amongst other things, shows that uncertainty provides a *raison d'être* for in-ventories. Chapter 5 looks at the consumption–savings decision and provides a simple exposition of a popular theory of portfolio choice.

The remainder of the book looks at less straightforward applica-tions. In fact many of these topics would be impossible to discuss without uncertainty. In Chapters 6 and 7 the analysis focuses on futures, insurance and stock markets. Chapter 8 studies problems that arise in markets where there is quality uncertainty surrounding the goods or services being traded. Finally in Chapter 9 I look at the modelling of the ways in which people gather information and hence I provide an introduction to an area of analysis known as search theory.

1. Markets in an Uncertain Environment

1.1 INTRODUCTION

This book is about microeconomics—the analysis of individual decisions and their market consequences. However, the treatment of the microeconomic issues differs from the treatment in many texts in that the agents make decisions in environments which are in some way uncertain.

The introduction of uncertainty both adds another level at which practically every area of microeconomic analysis may be studied, and contributes several new areas which would be impossible to study in the absence of uncertainty considerations. No branch of microeconomics has escaped the uncertainty treatment and the expansion of the subject into new areas has introduced new problems for the analysis of individual decision-makers and of market equilibrium. In the latter case especially, uncertainty causes serious problems of coordination in markets and it is apparent in some cases that the neoclassical 'price mechanism' may result in some peculiarities.

This chapter is an overview of the so-called economics of uncertainty. A brief reflection on the very many ways in which uncertainty enters our lives and effects our economic decisions makes clear that a full taxonomy of possible models is out of the question. The entire book is selective in its topics and it seems appropriate therefore to be selective in the discussion of this chapter. Wherever possible the illustrations I will use demonstrate fairly typical problems which arise in a wide variety of markets. However, to keep things concrete I will make the market for a consumption good, much favoured in microeconomic texts, the focal point of the discussion. In the following section I study how the problem of individual consumer choice may be affected by uncertainty. Section 1.3 raises some consequent issues of market equilibrium and allocative efficiency.

1.2 INDIVIDUAL DECISION-MAKING

In general three intimately related themes should concern us when considering how uncertainty may enter into individual decision-making. Firstly, what is the decision-maker uncertain about? Secondly, what form does the uncertainty take? Finally, what, if anything, may be done to act upon or to improve the information available?

I choose to discuss these considerations in the context of a model of consumer choice. Our point of departure is the familiar problem of choice of consumption bundle resulting from utility maximisation subject to a budget constraint. Recall that the individual chooses a combination of goods each of which is well defined, homogeneous and sells for a single known price. The individual's income available for expenditure on consumption is also known. Usually, the problem is couched in a *static* or single-period setting, but the dynamic problem, involving intertemporal choices, borrowing and savings opportunities is also available.

Now apply our three questions to this problem. What are the possibilities for the study of the consumer choice problem under uncertainty? To apply the first query, notice that the consumer could be uncertain about any one or any combination of the following: income, product price, product quality, product availability, and, in the dynamic setting, future income, interest rates and inflation rates. Already, we see many possibilities for the modelling of the uncertain consumer and, of course, there are more. It will be apparent in the remainder of the book that the uncertainty is usually taken to apply to only one or at most two key variables in the decision-maker's environment. This approach is adopted to keep the analysis simple and to discern the role played by particular variables in affecting changes in the results. Restricting the modelling of uncertainty in this way clearly contrasts with the incidence of uncertainty in everyday life, which is all-pervading. The proliferation of models under uncertainty arises because *any* feature of the certainty model may be taken as being subject to uncertainty and, for analytical reasons, it is best to relax the certainty assumption for one variable at a time. However, the application of the first of our questions raises few conceptual difficulties apart from the sheer numbers of possibilities. This is not the case with the other two questions.

By the 'form' of the uncertainty I mean the extent of our knowledge or ignorance. For example, we may decide to study uncertainty about product price in our consumer case. So price is 'uncertain', but what *do* we know about the product price? Surely we are not in complete ignorance? What does 'uncertain' mean? There are very many answers to this question and the importance of the topic easily justifies a volume or two for its discussion. For our purposes it is necessary only to suggest examples of types of uncertainty which occupy the vast grey area between certainty and ignorance.

Suppose there is uncertainty about the price of one of the goods that the consumer is hoping to buy, perhaps because some stores are offering discounts. It may be that 'experience' of the consumer and that of other consumers has produced an objective frequency distribution for prices from which we deduce that the probability of the consumer paying price p_i is q_i, (and $\sum q_i$), and the expected price to be paid or mean price is $\sum p_i q_i$. This appears to be the most straightforward specification of the problem and we make much use of it and generalisations of it throughout the book. However, despite introducing the flavour of there being an absence of certainty, the information required to construct an objectively given distribution for product prices is still formidable. Here are some alternatives.

(a) We do not know q_is but we may *order* probabilities so that for two prices p_i and p_j we may say that $q_i > q_j$ or $q_i < q_j$ or $q_i = q_j$. In this case, of course, the decision problem facing the consumer may not be resolved using the expected value calculation and some other decision criterion must be found.

(b) We do not know q_is for certain but we have subjective beliefs about the probability distribution. In this case we may choose to proceed *as if* our subjective probability distribution, q_is, were in fact the 'correct' one. This possibility raises a further complication to be discussed when we come to apply the third and final question.

(c) We make use, not of probabilities of finding particular prices but other weights, which do not necessarily behave as probabilities, reflecting our confidence or belief in finding particular prices.

(d) We do not make use of probabilities or weights of any kind because we have no prior information on which to base our beliefs. Notice that this is not pure ignorance—we are still assumed to know what the *prices* are.

Some of these alternative ways of capturing 'uncertainty' are discussed in the following chapter. Those which are not, and they include some very important ones, may be followed up in the references cited in this chapter's bibliographic guide.

The third question is really concerned with the constraints on individual behaviour given a particular informational environment. In the simplest case the 'static' problem of the certainty model may be carried over. In this case, whatever the form of the uncertainty the individual is the helpless victim of the uncertain environment and has only one opportunity to reach a decision. This has been referred to as decision-making in a *passive* situation. In our consumer example the individual takes a chance on being able to afford the preferred combination of goods. Many decision problems may be studied in this static or passive setting and frequent use is made of this method throughout the book.

However, few people are prepared to accept the consequences of uncertainty in a passive way. In our consumer example the individual is unlikely to settle for the first price if this is regarded as being 'high' and further stores may well be visited. Indeed, 'shopping' is a word which evokes the active process of visiting several stores in search of a single item. Decision-making in *active* situations therefore involves two decisions, at least. There is the decision of what to buy and that of how much shopping around should be undertaken. The latter is part of the economic problem because it uses time and resources but also has possible benefits in terms of widening the purchase opportunities beyond those offered by the passive approach. In Chapter 9 of this book an active problem known as search is discussed in some detail.

The modelling of uncertainty suggested under (b) above raises yet another type of opportunity for the decision-maker. In this case not only might the consumer shop around for the best buy, but time and resources may be spent in acquiring additional information for its own sake. That is, extra price quotes may be sought not simply as part of the quest for keeping expenditures to a minimum but in order that a clearer picture of opportunities is acquired and subjective prior beliefs updated in the light of information received. This ingredient is clearly absent from active decision-making based on objective probability assessments. This search for information *per se* may radically alter the individual's perception of the opportunities available and for this reason these decisions are referred to as resulting in *adaptive* behaviour.

Because active and adaptive behaviour in the context of the consumer model create a complex joint decision of both what to consume and how long to spend in search of the desired bundle we might choose to focus on the second decision alone. This is the approach adopted in many models away from the budget constraint problem and towards the constraints on and methods of search.

There are a large number of models of individual behaviour under uncertainty, many of which may be summarized using some of the terms introduced in this section. The models are invariably of interest, are often fascinating and occasionally produce unexpected results. However, some of the most challenging problems in the economics of uncertainty revolve around market equilibrium issues, and it is to some of these problems that we now turn.

1.3 MARKET EQUILIBRIUM AND EFFICIENCY

The possible consequences for marketing equilibrium under uncertainty are wide ranging and I confine attention to a few issues which arise most frequently.

Firstly there is the issue of how exchange takes place in an uncoordinated market. Under certainty we generally appeal to the myth of an auctioneer who brings traders together and determines the price at which trade takes place in the market so that excess demand is zero. The key role of the auctioneer is that of providing information and as such it is inappropriate that the auctioneer be carried over into markets with uncertainty. What does a market look like without an auctioneer? One problem is that price-setting is now a job for individual agents or groups of agents, and it is unlikely, therefore, that in the short run the prices chosen by agents, usually producers, based on their individual experience will be either identical or 'correct'. This produces, amongst other things the price uncertainty faced by consumers discussed in the previous section. How long and to what extent price differences are maintained depends critically both on the persistence of the searchers, and the behaviour of firms in adjusting prices in response to excess demands.

Secondly, there are the problems which arise when goods traded differ in their quality in a way that is not readily apparent merely by inspection. Quite often in these cases there are incentives for suppliers to release knowingly faulty goods onto the market and thereby exploit an informational advantage over consumers. Further, consumers are likely to be aware that suppliers could behave in this way but will be powerless to act directly on this because of the informational assymmetry. In this case the best course of action for consumers may be to expect the worst and treat all apparently identical commodities as being inferior. The problem is further exacerbated if the price at which supply is offered is an indicator of quality, with low prices indicating low quality. There is the possibility here that no price would be low enough (or all prices are 'too high') to tempt the consumer into a purchase. The difficulties of equilibrium in markets with quality uncertainty and assymmetric information are discussed in Chapters 7 and 8.

Finally there are problems with allocative efficiency in market equilibrium. If resources are used in order to counteract the effects of uncertainty what guarantees are there that the resources will be used efficiently? We have just outlined as example of extreme market failure—the possible non-existence of equilibrium. However, less extreme cases may arise because of, for example, informational externalities. A typical informational externality may arise in an active (search) decision environment. The uncovering of an opportunity by one consumer may easily benefit 'neighbouring' consumers who are relieved of the burden of undertaking a fresh search at full cost. In this example the external economy may result in 'too little' information-gathering by society as a whole.

There are several types of inefficiency encountered in information-deficient markets, some of which are illustrated in later chapters of this book.

1.4 CONCLUSION

This chapter has aimed to introduce quite general issues relating to individual decisions and the workings of markets under uncertainty using the vehicle of a theory of the consumer. Many examples of the uncertainty framework and the problems which arise are contained in the following chapters. Many more are not and the serious student must endeavour to follow up the selected references.

1.5 BIBLIOGRAPHIC GUIDE

A summary of approaches to uncertainty is provided in the following chapter. The distinction between passive, active and adaptive behaviour is introduced and followed up comprehensively in Hey (1981). For an early exposition of the consequences of uncertainty for market equilibrium the reader is encouraged to read Arrow (1959).

2. Approaches to Decision-making Under Uncertainty

2.1 INTRODUCTION

Under conditions of complete certainty, decisions result in certain consequences. The theory of the individual consumer choosing a particular consumption bundle is an example. The ingredients of the choice problem are the individual's preferences between goods, the income available and the prevailing product prices—all of which are known. In addition, the individual has a complete list of available goods from which to choose. The result of this choice problem is, therefore, a 'basket' of goods assembled in particular quantities. In a certain world there is no reason to distinguish between the choice of the basket and the act of consumption—the story finishes as soon as the decision is made. The decision and the outcome correspond perfectly.

Under uncertainty the consequences of a particular decision are not known for certain until the uncertainty is resolved by the passage of time. Take the consumer problem again. Having *decided* on an ideal basket of goods, under uncertainty that particular basket may not be available or available at 'unexpected' prices. Decision-making under uncertainty involves taking account, as best we can, of all the possible consequences of our actions. The ultimate level of utility we achieve will depend not only on which decision we make (as in the certainty case) but also on the way in which uncertainty is resolved or on which 'state of the world' obtains.

2.2 ACTS AND STATES

Consequences, in the form of ultimate outcomes, follow from a chosen act *and* the realisation of a particular state. Decision-making under uncertainty involves arriving at a decision in choosing a course of action before the state is realised. As an example, suppose you must decide today whether to visit a friend tomorrow. Ideally, you would like to know what the weather will be like because if it rains your journey will be rather unpleasant. Unfortunately, to give your friend warning you must decide today. The choice of action is between 'visit' and 'do not visit' while the states are 'rain', 'no rain'. The amount of satisfaction you receive depends both on your decision and on nature. Suppose the utilities associated with the act-state pairs are

visit/rain	¼
visit/no rain	1
do not visit/rain	½
do not visit/no rain	½

Clearly these may be arranged in a block or matrix.

	s_1 rain	s_2 no rain	
a_1 visit	¼	1	
a_2 do not visit	½	½	(2.1)

I have attached a value 1 to the most preferred outcome and ¼ to the least preferred. You may have different preferences depending on how much you like your friend and how little you like rain! The decision involves choosing between a_1 and a_2 before the state (either s_1 or s_2) is realised. Approaches to solving problems of this type are the subject of this and the following chapter. Applications to various 'economic' decisions are, of course, found in the rest of the book.

One difficulty I have overlooked thus far is that of the definition of *uncertainty* itself. One distinction is that under uncertainty we do not attach probabilities or likelihoods to the states of the world. In our example, we do not specify the likelihood of rain tomorrow. If we did introduce probabilities in this way the analysis would (according to this definition) be one involving *risk* rather than uncertainty. On this definition most of this book is not about uncertainty but about risk. Clearly I do not adhere to this distinction at all closely. To me, and many others uncertainty is a quite general term meaning 'absence of certainty'.

For the remainder of this chapter we will, on the whole,

disregard probabilities and see if there are sensible criteria for reaching decisions on courses of action. In subsequent chapters we will largely have the additional complexity of associated probabilities of states to consider.

2.3 DECISION CRITERIA

We will continue to consider a problem involving two actions and two states so that the *payoff matrix* has just four elements. Consider the following payoff matrix, the elements of which you may think of as 'utilities' or money amounts.

	s_1	s_2
a_1	6	7
a_2	5	10

$$(2.2)$$

How would *you* choose between a_1 and a_2? Several possible criteria have been suggested.

(i) *Maximin*. Using this criterion we look at the worst possible outcome associated with each action and choose that action with the largest minimum payoff. In our example the minimum payoff associated with a_1 is 6 while that associated with a_2 is 5. Using the maximin rule we choose a_1. Notice that this rule implies a very pessimistic view of things. For example, we disregard entirely the fact that by choosing a_2 we face the *possibility* of receiving 10.

(ii) *Minimax*. This takes the form of a *regret* criterion focusing on the opportunity cost of each action. To see this we transform the matrix in (2.2) into its regret equivalent. Suppose we chose action a_1 and state s_1 occurred. Clearly we would not regret this move since we receive 6 while had we selected a_2 we would receive only 5. Hence, the regret factor is zero. Suppose, however, that we had chosen a_1 and state s_2 occurred. In this case we receive 7 but had we chosen a_2 we would have received 10 and so the opportunity cost or regret factor is the difference between what we have and what we might have had, 3. This gives us the first row of our regret matrix. The second row has a similar construction.

The regret matrix is therefore;

$$
\begin{array}{ccc}
 & s_1 & s_2 \\
a_1 & 0 & 3 \\
a_2 & 1 & 0
\end{array}
\tag{2.3}
$$

The minimax rule tells us to look at the maximum regret associated with each action and choose that action with the smallest maximum regret factor. In this example the maximum regret associated with a_1 is 3 while that associated with a_2 is only 1—hence we choose a_2.

(iii) *Maximax*. If maximin reflects extreme pessimism, the maximax rule reflects extreme optimism. In this case we only look at the maximum return associated with each action and choose that action with the largest maximum return. On this criterion we choose a_2 in (2.2).

Before continuing with yet more decision criteria we should question the reasonableness of these, the most basic, rules.

Consider the following payoff matrix:

$$
\begin{array}{ccc}
 & s_1 & s_2 \\
a_1 & 0 & 200 \\
a_2 & 0.5 & 0.5
\end{array}
\tag{2.4}
$$

The maximin rule chooses action a_2. Would you make the same choice? Probably you would not. Now look at the associated regret matrix in (2.5)

$$
\begin{array}{ccc}
 & s_1 & s_2 \\
a_1 & 0.5 & 0 \\
a_2 & 0 & 199.5
\end{array}
\tag{2.5}
$$

The minimax rule chooses a_1. Returning to (2.4) the maximax rule selects a_1 also. Would you regard this as a reckless choice?

Clearly the choice of rule will depend to some extent on what is at stake. The extreme caution of the maximin rule may be appropriate when choosing between nuclear-generated and hydro-generated power, but seems unreasonable when losses are negligible and gains very large, as in (2.4).

These simple rules are rather rigid, focusing on only one type of payoff and ignoring other information present in the payoff matrix. Other decision rules attempt to correct for this deficiency.

(iv) *Hurwicz rule*. This rule associates with each action a_1 an index $h(a_i)$, which is a weighted average of the minimum and maximum payoffs associated with each action. The action with the largest $h(.)$ index is selected. Using the payoffs in (2.2) the indices are:

$$h(a_1) = \alpha 6 + (1 - \alpha) \quad 7$$

$$h(a_2) = \alpha 5 + (1 - \alpha) \quad 10 \qquad (2.6)$$

where $0 \leqq \alpha \leqq 1$. The selection made by this rule depends critically on the value of α which is decided upon by the individual decision-maker. Observe that if $\alpha = 1$ the Hurwicz rule makes the same choice as the maximin rule while if $\alpha = 0$ we select the same action as the maximax rule. In view of this α is often referred to as the pessimism–optimism index. As α varies between 0 and 1 the relative attractiveness of each course of action also varies. This is illustrated in Figure 2.1. If $\alpha = 0$, $h(a_1) = 7$ while $h(a_2) = 10$, hence we choose a_2 (as we did with the ultra-optimistic maximax rule). If $\alpha = 1$, $h(a_1) = 6$ and $h(a_2) = 5$ and we choose a_1 (as we did with the ultra-pessimistic maximin rule). Plotting out the two equations in (2.6) we see that as long as $\alpha < 0.75$ we choose a_2, while we choose a_1 if $\alpha > 0.75$. It is clear from the diagram (and by solving the two equations in (2.6)) that we would be indifferent between a_1 and a_2 if $\alpha = 0.75$.

The Hurwicz criterion seems to avoid the undesirable implication of the simple rules of being guided only by extremes. As long as we are confident about our choice of α the rule appears to be reasonable.

However, there appear to be two difficulties with the Hurwicz criterion. The first is evident from Figure 2.1. The choice of action may well be sensitive to choice of α—in our example this is particularly true for values of α in the neighbourhood of 0.75. The second is a largely logical difficulty, and involves the resolution of indifference. If your α-value in the last example were 0.75 you

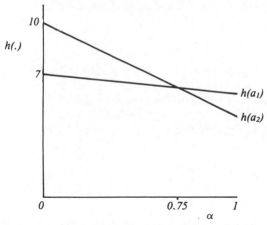

Figure 2.1: Hurwicz indices

would be indifferent between each action and hence unable to choose. Presumably you would be happy to see the choice be determined by the toss of a fair coin—a common way of resolving harmless deadlocks. Thus, in addition to the two actions, a_1 and a_2 there is a random action which involves pursuing a_1 half the time and a_2 for the other half. This is often referred to as a *mixed* strategy. In terms of (2.2) the additional possibility of a randomised action, a_3 produces:

	s_1	s_2	
a_1	6	7	
a_2	5	10	
$a_3 \equiv (0.5a_1, 0.5a_2)$	5.5	8.5	(2.7)

Suppose we use the Hurwicz criterion and let our choice be determined by the largest $h(.)$ index. Let $\alpha = 0.75$, which we know makes us indifferent between a_1 and a_2. We have,

$$h(a_1) = 0.75(6) + 0.25(7) = 6.25$$
$$h(a_2) = 0.75(5) + 0.25(10) = 6.25$$
$$h(a_3) = 0.75(5.5) + 0.25(8.5) = 6.25 \qquad (2.8)$$

which confirms that we would be happy using the mixed strategy a_3 as a means of resolving our indifference because $h(a_3)$ is no less than $h(a_1)$ or $h(a_2)$. This seems reasonable and is not unexpected.

However, consider the following and let $\alpha = 0.25$.

	s_1	s_2	
a_1	0	1	
a_2	1	0	
$a_3 \equiv (0.5a_1, 0.5a_2)$	0.5	0.5	(2.9)

In this case, $h(a_1) = 0.75$, $h(a_2) = 0.75$ (hence we are indifferent between a_1 and a_2), but $h(a_3) = 0.375$, and so we would not be prepared to see this outcome determined by the toss of a coin. Do you think this is reasonable? How *would* you resolve the indecision?

The idea of attaching *weights* to outcomes will be pursued further in the next chapter where we will suggest ways in which the weights are constructed so as to minimise 'unreasonable' behaviour.

(v) *The principle of insufficient reason.* One objection to the criteria discussed so far is that the likelihood of each state of the world occurring is ignored. On the contrary most people find it irresistible to think of likelihoods of events. Returning to an earlier example, suppose s_1 and s_2 were associated with 'rain tomorrow' and 'no rain tomorrow', even if we are reluctant to attach probabilities to each outcome we would usually be willing to say which outcome we thought the more likely. Our assessment would be based on information from a variety of sources including today's weather conditions, past experience and professional forecasts. On the strict definition of uncertainty we are unable to form probability statements. The 'principle of insufficient reason' suggests that under such circumstances all states of the world should be considered equally likely. If you feel that you must attach probabilities to states but have no reason to regard any one probability distribution as being appropriate, assume that the states are equally likely.

The decision criterion resulting from this principle is that the preferred action is the one yielding the greatest *expected* outcome. Consider once again the problem in (2.2) but now associate with each state the same probability of occurrence (of course, the sum of the probabilities must be 1).

	s_1	s_2	
	(0.5)	(0.5)	
a_1	6	7	
a_2	5	10	(2.10)

Denote by $E(a_i)$ the expected value of action i. These are:

$$E(a_1) = 0.5(6) + 0.5(7) = 6.5$$

$$E(a_2) = 0.5(5) + 0.5(10) = 7.5 \qquad (2.11)$$

On this basis the second action is chosen. Hence, the expected value indices of the principle of insufficient reason play the same role as the h-indices of the Hurwicz criterion, and both are weighted averages of the outcomes. However, whereas the weights determining the h-indices are subjectively chosen, those associated with the expected values are forced by the acceptance of the principle of insufficient reason. I return to this briefly in section 2.5.

2.4 DECISIONS AND GAMES

So far we have looked at the choice of action in the face of an uncertain environment summarised as alternative 'states of the world'. Most decision problems in this book are of this type. However, suppose that rather than choosing actions when ultimate consequences are determined by the course of 'nature' they result from decisions made by yourself and another decision-maker. This, of course, constitutes a *game*. In this case the 'opponent' is not an impartial 'nature' but a self-seeking individual trying to make the best of things—just like you! Your opponent will be making decisions in anticipation of your decision and you will attempt to anticipate your opponent in your choice of action. Most card games and chess are examples of 'games' of this type.

The theory of games is a fascinating branch of decision-making with many interesting applications to economics. The aim here is not to review or even to outline this extensive area, but it seems useful to illustrate the interesting problems that arise when modelling interdependent decisions. The following well-known example is often known as the *Prisoner's Dilemma*.

Suppose two prisoners are held in separate cells on suspicion of a robbery to which neither accused has confessed. Each prisoner faces two possible actions: 'confess' or 'not confess' (escape and suicide are ruled out!). Each prisoner is approached in turn and made a proposition. If a prisoner makes a confession which implicates the other the prosecution is prepared to allow a deal in which the confessant is given a token sentence of three months while the other is given the maximum term of ten years. Everybody knows that if they both confess there is no possibility of a deal that will discriminate between them although the courts may show some leniency and give both a reduced sentence of eight years. On the other hand, since there is little other evidence to convict for the full crime, if neither confesses the police (in possession of little evidence on the main charge) prosecute for a minor offence for which both prisoners receive one year. The 'payoff' matrix is as follows:

		prisoner 2	
		confess	do not confess
		(a_1)	(a_2)
	confess (a_1)	(8 yrs, 8yrs)	(3 mths, 10 yrs)
prisoner 1	do not confess (a_2)	(10 yrs, 3 mths)	(1 yr, 1 yr)

$$(2.12)$$

The first number in each element is prisoner 1's punishment and the second is prisoner 2's punishment. Now, remembering that the prisoners are isolated from each other and hence are unable to co-operate what decision will be made by each prisoner? Consider the first prisoner. The maximin strategy would result in action a_1 being selected. However, a_1 is a maximin choice for the second prisoner, so that each prisoner independently pursuing a maximin strategy produces the undesirable outcome of eight years in prison for each. Neither prisoner has any incentive to anticipate maximin behaviour of the other by choosing not to confess. If both prisoners could cooperate they would probably both choose not to confess (although each runs the risk of the other cheating), but without such cooperation it is not individually rational for either to make this choice. The maximin action may be individually rational but 'socially' undesirable—hence the dilemma.

2.5   CONCLUSION

In this chapter we have outlined a variety of rules which may be used to arrive at choices in an uncertain environment. Further, the ultimate outcomes of choices—the elements of the payoff matrices—were (by and large) capable of being interpreted either as money amounts or 'utility' levels.

In the following chapter we take matters further forward in two respects.. Firstly, we allow for the states of the world to have probabilities of occurrence associated with them, so that we move into a world of risk. Thus, either based on past experience or on subjective evaluation, we are able to say that state s_1 occurs with probability p_1 and s_2 with probability p_2. Clearly, this is not unconnected with some of the ideas of section 2.3. If p_1 and p_2 are regarded as degrees of opimism or pessimism as appropriate then we are in the Hurwicz world. If $p_1 = p_2 = 0.5$ then our behaviour will have the same effect as the principle of insufficient reason. With p_1 and p_2 as (not necessarily equal) probabilities and interpreting the elements of the matrix in (2.2) as money amounts we may calculate the expected payoff of each action as:

$$E(a_1) = p_1 \quad 6 + p_2 \quad 7$$

$$E(a_2) = p_1 \quad 5 + p_2 \quad 10 \qquad (2.13)$$

where $p_1 + p_2 = 1$.

If we choose our action according to the highest expected payoff our choice will depend on the values we assign to p_1 and p_2. Suppose we believe that $p_1 = 0.22$ and $p_2 = 0.78$, then $E(a_1) = 6.78$ and $E(a_2) = 8.90$ and we choose action a_2. This *expected value* criterion has the advantage of weighting the various outcomes and of insuring that the weights are likelihoods associated with states. However, it has a disadvantage, which is that our level of satisfaction or utility particularly in risky situations may not be matched one-for-one by the monetary gains. For example, diminishing marginal utility of money is not allowed for.

As the second development in the next chapter we examine the problem of associating a utility measure with monetary gains. As we will see, care must be taken so that our choice of utility measure leads us to make consistent choice patterns.

2.6 BIBLIOGRAPHIC GUIDE

Decision criteria are considered more formally in Luce and Raiffa (1957) (ch. 13 sections 13.1 to 13.3) where there is also an exposition of the Prisoner's Dilemma (ch. 5 section 5.4). Applications of some of these criteria to actual decision problems may be found in Moore and Thomas (1976) and Moore *et al.* (1976). Some historical and philosophical background is contained in Arrow (1951).

2.7 EXERCISES

2.1 Consider the following payoff matrix where the numbers are 'utility' payoffs.

	s_1	s_2	s_3
a_1	0	10	2
a_2	3	4	0
a_3	2	0	9

Which action is selected by:
(a) the maximin criterion
(b) the minimax regret criterion
(c) the Hurwicz rule with $\alpha = 0.75$
(d) the principle of insufficient reason.

2.2 Suppose the matrix in question 2.1 is extended by the introduction of a randomised action $a_4 = 0.5\, a_1 + 0.5\, a_3$. Does this affect any of the choices? What is your interpretation of a_4 as a 'randomised action'?

2.3 Using the Hurwicz rule in question 2.1, what value of α makes you indifferent between a_1 and a_3?

3. Expected Utility Theory

3.1 INTRODUCTION

In the last chapter we characterised uncertainty in such a way that a chosen course of action by a decision-maker resulted not in a single outcome but in a range of possible outcomes weighted by their probabilities of occurence—a lottery. Several ways of deciding on a particular course of action were put forward including one which suggested selection based on maximising the *expected money value* of the action.

For example, consider two alternative courses of action resulting in the following alternative lotteries:

$$L^1 = [(0.2, 50), (0.6, 25), (0.2, 10)] \qquad (3.1)$$

$$L^2 = [(0.3, 50), (0.4, 25), (0.3, 10)] \qquad (3.2)$$

The expected value of L^1 is 27 while that of L^2 is 28, making L^2 the winner. But look again at the two lotteries. Is L^2 really better than L^1? A comparison between (3.1) and (3.2) may involve many considerations other than expected money value. Here are two.

1. L^2 is better because of the increased chance of gaining 50.
2. L^2 is less desirable because of the increased chance of gaining only 10.

Either way your *feelings* about L^1 and L^2 might not be accurately summarised by the expected value calculation.

This chapter develops a theory which allows our feelings or attitudes towards risky choices to be characterised in a consistent way. The theory we develop is quite general (for example, we do not need the outcomes to be expressed in money terms) but in the remainder of this section we highlight the need for such a theory by considering only fair lotteries with just two money outcomes. A *fair* lottery or gamble is one in which there is an equal chance of each outcome occurring. Consider the following two lotteries:

$$L^3 = [(0.5, 50), (0.5, 10)] \qquad (3.3)$$

$$L^4 = [(0.5, \ 30), \ (0.5, \ 30)] \qquad (3.4)$$

Both lotteries have the same expected payoff. Are you indifferent between them? Probably not, because L^4 pays out 30 for sure while L^3 has an expected payoff of 30, being an average of 50 and 10. One good test of how you feel about lotteries is to ask how much money at the most you would pay in order to face a particular lottery. The very most you would pay for L^4 ought to be 30 (why?). But would you pay out 30 for L^3? Probably not, even though on average L^3 pays out 30. In this case your feelings about L^3 and L^4 are not accurately summarized in the expected value calculation.

The following fair lottery takes this idea to its extreme. The lottery involves the repeated toss of a fair coin. If the coin lands showing tails at any stage the game ends and you receive nothing. For as long as the game continues if the coin lands showing heads you receive (2^n) where n is the number of times the coin has landed showing heads. Hence, the probability of winning 4 is ¼ [the probability of the game 'surviving' the first toss (½) × the probability of a head on the second toss (½)], the probability of winning 8 is ⅛ and so on. The expected money value of the game is:

$$(2 \times \tfrac{1}{2}) + (4 \times \tfrac{1}{4}) + (8 \times \tfrac{1}{8}) + \dots$$
$$= 1 + 1 + 1 \dots. \qquad = \infty \qquad (3.5)$$

The expected value of the lottery is infinite, but nobody would pay such an amount to face this lottery, and most of us would pay a relatively small amount! This problem, known as the *St Petersburg Paradox*, shows the weakness of expected money value as a criterion for summarising our feelings about lotteries.

Misgivings about the expected payoff criterion in all the lotteries discussed so far in this chapter have a common origin. We feel that the expected payoff gives insufficient attention to extreme outcomes. All of us would probably agree that the chances of finishing with nothing are given inadequate weight in the St Petersburg problem, and many of us to a lesser or greater extent feel the same about lotteries L^1, L^2 and L^3. Clearly there is scope for a method of choosing between lotteries which takes account of these factors. In the following section I show that a consistent way of choosing between lotteries exists if a set of axioms is obeyed. I will set up the axiom system and prove an important hypothesis. In subsequent sections I will give examples of how the system works, what it means and how robust it is as a predictor of choice patterns.

3.2 THE EXPECTED UTILITY HYPOTHESIS

I will assume that there are just four possible outcomes to be thought of as money amounts $y_i(i = 1, \ldots, 4)$. The structure of the hypothesis is applicable for any finite number of outcomes.

Axiom 1: There is a complete and transitive preference—ordering over outcomes.

(i) For y_i and y_j either

$$y_i \succsim y_j \text{ (read '}y_i \text{ is preferred or indifferent to } y_j\text{')}$$

or

$$y_j \succsim y_i \text{ (read '}y_j \text{ is preferred or indifferent to } y_i\text{').}$$

(ii) If $y_i \succsim y_j$ and $y_j \succsim y_i$ then $y_i \sim y_j$.
(iii) If $y_i \succsim y_j$ and $y_j \succsim y_k$ then $y_i \succsim y_k$.
(iv) If $y_i \succsim y_j$ then $y_i \geqq y_j$ (more is preferred to less).

I will assume that $y_1 \geqq y_2 \geqq y_3 \geqq y_4$ with $y_1 > y_4$ so that from (iv) above, $y_1 \succsim y_2 \succsim y_3 \succsim y_4$ with $y_1 \succ y_4$.

A lottery is written $L = [\{p_i, y_i\} i = 1, \ldots, 4]$. That is, a lottery is a set of pairs of outcomes with their associated probability of occurrence such that $p_i \geqq 0$, $i = 1, \ldots, 4$ and $\sum_{i=1}^{4} p_i = 1$. All outcomes are mutually exclusive.

Axiom 2: For any lotteries there is an ordering which is complete and transitive.

(i) Either

$$L^i \succsim L^j \text{ or } L^j \succsim L^i$$

(ii) If $L^i \succsim L^j$ and $L^j \succsim L^k$ then $L^i \succsim L^k$

The essence of the problem is to find a criterion by which we can say for *any* lotteries, which is preferred and hence which out of a given collection of lotteries will be chosen.

Axiom 3: Consider a lottery including only y_1 and y_4—the largest and the smallest outcomes. For any y_i there exists a number u_i between 0 and 1 such that the outcome y_i is equally preferred to a lottery involving y_1 with probability $(1 - u_i)$. Such a lottery is said to be a *standard lottery* for y_i, L_i^*. Hence,

$$L_i^* \equiv [u_i y_1, (1 - u_i)y_4] \sim y_i$$

Note that u_i is not the probability that y_i occurs. It is the probability with which y_i would have to occur to make the individual indifferent between y_i and a lottery involving only y_1 and y_4. In fact, u_i is a *subjective* evaluation made by an individual. More of this will be discussed later.

Clearly we must have,

$$L_1^* \equiv [1.y_1, 0.y_4] \sim y_1 \quad \text{so that} \quad u_1 = 1$$

and

$$L_4^* \equiv [0.y_1, 1.y_4] \sim y_4 \quad \text{so that} \quad u_4 = 0$$

Now consider the standard lottery for y_2.

$$L_2^* \equiv [u_2 y_1, (1 - u_2)y_4] \sim y_2$$

since $y_2 \leq y_1$ we must have no greater weight attached to y_1 in L_2^* than was attached to y_1 in L_1^*. Hence, $u_2 \leq u_1$ and similarly for

$$L_3^* \equiv [u_3 y_1, (1 - u_3)y_4] \sim y_3$$

we require $u_3 \leq u_2$ giving the complete order of

$$u_1 \geq u_2 \geq u_3 \geq u_4 \qquad u_1 = 1, \ u_4 = 0.$$

For each y_i there is one and only one u_i. This is important and we capitalise on this later.

Axiom 4: Suppose there is some equally preferred alternative to y_3, say x, *which may be a lottery*. Then since $y_3 \sim x$ an individual should be indifferent between two lotteries L^1 and L^2 if the only difference between them is that where L^1 contains y_3, L^2 contains x.

For example, if

$$L^1 = [(p_1, y_1), (p_2, y_2), (p_3, y_3), (p_4, y_4)]$$

and

$$L^2 = [(p_1, y_1), (p_2, y_2), (p_3, x), (p_4, y_4)]$$

then $x \sim y_3$ implies $L^1 \sim L^2$.

Further, if for two lotteries, L^1 as above and L^3 given by:

$$L^3 = [(1 - p_3, y_2), (p_3, x)]$$

then the choice between L^1 and L^3 is independent of y_3 and x.

Axiom 5: Suppose there is a lottery L_1 which has other lotteries as outcomes L^1, L^2 with associated probabilities q^1 and q^2 respectively. (Of course $q^2 = 1 - q^1$ but I will keep the notation distinct to make the generalisation clearer.) L^1 and L^2 in turn have y_is as outcomes as before. Hence,

$$L_1 = [\{q^j, L^j\} j = 1, 2]$$

while

$$L^j = [\{p_i^j, y_i\} i = 1, \ldots, 4] \qquad j = 1, 2.$$

Now consider the choice between L_1 and

$$L_2 = [\{p_i, y_i\} i = 1, \ldots, 4]$$

Expanding L_1 so that it is expressed in terms of the ultimate outcomes we have,

$$L_1 = [([q^1 p_1^1 + q^2 p_1^2], y_1), ([q^1 p_2^1 + q^2 p_2^2], y_2),$$
$$([q^1 p_3^1 + q^2 p_3^2], y_3), ([q^1 p_4^1 + q^2 p_4^2], y_4)]$$

Hence, $L_1 \sim L_2$ if

$$p_i = \sum_{j=1}^{2} p_i^j q^j \qquad \text{each } i = 1, \ldots, 4$$

Axiom 6: If

$$L^1 = [(p, y_1), (1 - p, y_4)]$$

and

$$L^2 = [(q, y_1), (1 - q, y_4)]$$

then $L^1 \succsim L^2$ if and only if $p \geqq q$.

Before elaborating on these axioms and before we question their validity, I will derive the main result of this chapter, known as the *expected utility hypothesis*.

The expected utility of a lottery, L with outcomes y_i occurring with probabilities p_i is $U(L) = \sum_{i=1}^{4} p_i u_i$. The preferred lottery is one which has the greatest expected utility.

The structure of the proof is very simple and involves finding, for *any* lottery L^j, an equally preferred lottery involving only y_1 and y_4. The comparison among any lotteries then simply amounts to the comparison of the weight on y_1. By Axiom 6, the lottery with the largest weight on y_1 is preferred.

From Axiom 3 an outcome y_i is indifferent to its associated standard lottery $L_i^* = [u_iy_1, (1 - u_i)y_4]$. Thus in the lottery

$$L^1 = [\{p_i, y_i\}, i = 1, \ldots, 4]$$

each y_i may be replaced by its standard lottery giving the lottery

$$L^{1*} = [\{p_i, L_i^*\}, i = 1, \ldots, 4]$$

By Axiom 4 the individual should be indifferent between L^1 and L^{1*}. Expanding L^{1*} as with the procedure in Axiom 5 to arrive at the final outcomes y_1 and y_4 we have

$$L^{1*} = [([p_1u_1 + p_2u_2 + p_3u_3 + p_4u_4], y_1),$$

$$(p_1(1 - u_1) + p_2(1 - u_2) + p_3(1 - u_3) + p_4(1 - u_4)], y_4)]$$

$$= [(p, y_1, (1 - p), y_4)] \quad \text{where } p = \sum_{i=1}^{4} p_iu_i$$

Hence,

$$L^1 \sim [(p, y_1), (1 - p, y_4)] \quad \text{if } p = \sum_{i=1}^{4} p_iu_i$$

Similarly suppose there is another lottery L^2 with the same possible outcome as L^1 but with a different probability distribution over outcomes,

$$L^2 = [\{q_i, y_i\}, i = 1, \ldots, 4]$$

Using a similar application of the axioms as before we arrive at

$$L^2 \sim [(q, y_1), (1 - q, y_4)] \quad \text{if } q = \sum_{i=1}^{4} q_iu_i$$

Finally, by Axiom 6

$$L^1 \succsim L^2 \quad \text{if and only if} \quad p \geqq q.$$

Consider the index u_i. As derived, this is a weight associated by the decision-maker with a reward of y_i and for each y_i there is one and only one value of u_i. We may, therefore, define a function u which takes each money value of y and transforms it into an index (between 0 and 1) expressing the value to the decision-maker of a money amount y. The value to the decision-maker of a certain amount y is known as the *ex post* utility of y. The function transforming the y_is into u_is may be written $u(y)$ so that $u_i = u(y_i)$ and is called the *ex post* utility function. On the other hand, the *ex ante* utility is the expected utility of the outcomes y_i and their associated probabilities of occurrence. In our case of just four possible outcomes the expected utility of the lottery L^1 is

$$U(L^1) = \sum_{i=1}^{4} p_i u(y_i) = p$$

while the expected utility of L^2 is

$$U(L^2) = \sum_{i=1}^{4} q_i u(y_i) = q$$

Hence the ordering of lotteries is achieved by the ordering of expected utilities since

$$L^1 \succsim L^2 \quad \text{if and only if} \quad p \geqq q$$

and

$$p \geqq q \quad \text{implies} \quad U(L^1) \geqq U(L^2)$$

This is the essence of the expected utility hypothesis. The result may be derived for any number of outcomes y_i and any number of associated lotteries L^j. I will discuss this result and the importance of the axioms presently. First, an example may be instructive.

3.3 EXPECTED UTILITY IN ACTION

We started this chapter in some difficulty in choosing between two lotteries (3.1) and (3.2). The calculus of the expected utility hypothesis ought to help. In keeping with the notation developed in the last section suppose we have three possible outcomes;

$$y_1 = 50 \qquad y_2 = 25 \qquad y_3 = 10$$

Consider first lottery L^1, recall that this is,

$$L^1 = [(0.2, 50), (0.6, 25), (0.2, 10)]$$

We now take each y_i, in turn and derive the associated standard lottery L_i^*.

$$L_1^* = [u_1 50, (1 - u_1)10] \sim 50 \quad \text{implies} \quad u_1 = 1$$
$$L_3^* = [u_3 50, (1 - u_3)10] \sim 10 \quad \text{implies} \quad u_3 = 0$$

These are obvious enough but what about u_2?

$$L_2^* = [u_2 50, (1 - u_2)10]] \sim 25.$$

There is no obvious answer to this and any answer I may suggest may or may not be in agreement with yours. We are being asked for our feelings on this matter. Recall that u_i is a value a person chooses in order to make an outcome of u_i indifferent to its standard lottery. As such u_i will vary from person to person. We will see later that choosing a u_i amounts to revealing preferences about money values. For myself, u_2 would have to be around 0.6 so I write

$$L_2^* = [u_2 50, (1 - u_2)10] \sim 25 \quad \text{implies (for C. J. McKenna)}$$
$$u_2 = 0.6.$$

Now we substitute for each y_i in L^1 the associated standard lottery to give

$$L^{1*} = [(0.2, [50]), (0.6, [0.6(50) + 0.4(10)]), (0.2, [10])]$$
$$= [(0.56, 50), (0.44, 10)] \quad \text{and so } p = 0.56$$

A similar substitution into L^2 transforms

$$L^2 = [(0.3, 50), (0.4, 25), (0.3, 10)]$$

into

$$L^{2*} = [(0.3, [50]), (0.4, [0.6(50) + 0.4(10)]), (0.3, [10])]$$
$$= [(0.54, 50), (0.46, 10)] \quad \text{and so } q = 0.54$$

From the expected utility hypothesis we know that

$$L^1 \succsim L^2 \quad \text{if} \quad L^{1*} \succsim L^{2*}$$

and

$$L^{1*} \succsim L^{2*} \quad \text{if} \quad p \geqq q \quad \text{or} \quad U(L^1) \geqq U(L^2)$$

In this case we have

$$U(L^1) \equiv p = \sum_{i=1}^{3} p_i u_i = \sum_{i=1}^{3} p_i u(y_i) = 0.56$$

and

$$U(L^2) \equiv q = \sum_{i=1}^{3} q_i u_i = \sum_{i=1}^{3} q_i u(y_i) = 0.54$$

Apparently, I prefer L^1 to L^2. Lottery L^1 gives me a (slightly) higher utility than L^2. However, the race is a close one, and to see why suppose my choice of u_2 had been 0.5. It is easy to check that in this case I would be indifferent between L^1 and L^2 since

$U(L^1) = U(L^2) = 0.5$. If my choice of u_2 had been 0.4 my original preference would be reversed because in this case $U(L^1) = 0.44$ while $U(L^2) = 0.46$, making $U(L^1) < U(L^2)$.

In fact my choice of u_2 is resolving the debate we had in comparing L^1 and L^2. In selecting a low value of u_2 I would be tending more towards the first argument that 'L^2 is better because of the increased chance of gaining 50'. By selecting a high value of u_2 I am tending more towards the view that 'L^2 is less desirable because of the increased chance of gaining only 10'. Hence, an apparently complicated choice problem has been resolved quite simply—as long as we obey the six axioms.

As another example consider the problem of choosing between the lotteries in (3.3) and (3.4). Here again there are three possible outcomes

$$y_1 = 50 \qquad y_2 = 30 \qquad y_3 = 10$$

and we may rewrite (3.3) and (3.4) as

$$L^3 = [(0.5, 50), (0.0, 30), (0.5, 10)]$$
$$L^4 = [(0.0, 50), (1.0, 30), (0.0, 10)]$$

The choice is between a certainty of gaining 30 and a fair gamble with an expected money gain of 30.

As before set $u_1 = u(50) = 1$ and $u_3 = u(10) = 0$. The standard lottery for y_2 is

$$L_2^* = [u_2 50, (1 - u_2)10] \sim 30$$

You may have different ideas, but I would want more than a 50 per cent chance of gaining 50 in this lottery, say $u_2 = 0.7$. Hence,

$$L^{3*} = [(0.5, [50]), (0.0, [0.7(50) + 0.3(10)]), (0.4, [10])]$$

while

$$L^{4*} = [(0.0, [50]), (1.0, [0.7(50) + 0.3(10)]), (0.0, [10])]$$

giving

$$U(L^3) \equiv p = \sum_{i=1}^{3} p_i u(y_i) = 0.5$$

$$U(L^4) \equiv q = \sum_{i=1}^{3} q_i u(y_i) = 0.7$$

Therefore, I prefer the certainty of winning 30 to a fair gamble involving an expected money return of 30. Apparently, I dislike taking chances. As with the previous example this is revealed through my choice of u_2, and, once more, variations in my choice of u_2 will result in different preference rankings of lotteries. See for yourself what happens in this example if I had chosen $u_2 = 0.5$ or alternatively $u_2 = 0.4$ instead (Exercise 3.1).

3.4 THE NATURE OF THE UTILITY INDICES

Consider first the *ex post* utility function $u(y)$, which associates with any certain outcome y a number u expressing how one feels about the sum of money involved. Expressed this way it appears as if we have discovered a *cardinal utility* measure. The theory apparently depends on *ex post* utilities taking particular values. It is not sufficient that for two outcomes y_i and y_j that we merely prefer one to another but we must stipulate *how much* more we prefer one to the other in utility terms. It turns out, however, that what matters is not an absolute measure of utility (we are not revealing absolute degrees of satisfaction) but the calibration of a particular range of utility values to express our feelings about each outcome relative to the others. To see why, recall how the function $u(y)$ is structured.

Faced with a given range of possible outcomes, the largest is associated with a utility value of 1 and the smallest with a utility value of 0. In the first example of the last section the choice between lotteries L^1 and L^2 was arrived at by (amongst other things) assigning a utility value of 0 to the money value of 10. Does this mean I would obtain no utility from gaining 10? Clearly it does not. What matters when choosing between lotteries is not the utility values but the intermediate utility values *relative* to the selected interval, in this case (0, 1). This interval was selected so that we have an interpretation as a (subjective) probability weight in the standard lottery and makes the scaling or calibration of the interval fairly straightforward. However, what matters when choosing lotteries is the ranking of *ex ante* utilities or expected utilities $U(L)$. If we choose an interval other than (0, 1) for our utility measure we will leave the ultimate ranking of expected utility unchanged as long as the relative positions of the assigned utility numbers in the scale are unchanged.

For example, in choosing between L^1 and L^2 in section 3.3 the utility values assigned were 1 (for $y_1 = 50$), 0.6 (for $y_2 = 25$) and 0 (for $y_3 = 10$). But what mattered was not that $u(y_2) = 0.6$ but that $u(y_2) = 0.6$ *given that* $u(y_1) = 1$ and $u(y_3) = 0$. If the position of $u(y_2)$ *relative* to the maximum and minimum utility values is preserved the ultimate ranking of lotteries according to expected utility will also be preserved. The scale of utilities in this example may be changed as long as the ratio

$$\frac{u(25) - u(10)}{u(50) - u(25)} \tag{3.6}$$

is kept constant. Thus the values of $u(y_i)$ can be changed without affecting final preferences between lotteries as long as the utility ratio (3.6) is unaffected.

Consider (3.6); at the moment this has a value of

$$\frac{0.6 - 0.0}{1.0 - 0.6} = \frac{0.6}{0.4} = 1.5 \tag{3.7}$$

which means that we can transform our utility scale as long as the difference between $u(25)$ and $u(10)$ is 1.5 times the difference between $u(50)$ and $u(25)$, and no harm will come to the preference ordering based on expected utility.

For example, let us change the range of utility values from $(0, 1)$ to $(6, 7)$—by adding 6 to the lowest and highest utility score. Then, (3.6) will only remain unchanged if 6 is also added to the intermediate utility value, so that

$$\frac{6.6 - 6.0}{7.0 - 6.6} = 1.5$$

Similarly, doubling the interval from $(0, 1)$ to $(0, 2)$ leaves (3.6) unchanged if the intermediate value is also doubled from 0.6 to 1.2.

In fact any linear operation on the u-values will leave (3.6) unchanged. Hence, if we define a new *ex post* utility measure as

$$v(y_i) = a + bu(y_i) \qquad \text{all } i \tag{3.8}$$

so that v is a *linear transformation* of the function u then using v will lead us to the same choice of lotteries as did u. Suppose a and b in (3.8) take the values 6 and 2 respectively, then the expected utility of L^1 is now given by

$$V(L^1) = 0.2v(y_1) + 0.6v(y_2) + 0.2v(y_3)$$
$$= 0.2[6 + 2u(50)] + 0.6[6 + 2u(25)] + 0.2[6 + 2u(10)]$$
$$= 0.2[8] + 0.6[7.2] + 0.2[6]$$
$$= 7.12$$

while that of L^2 is given by

$$V(L^2) = 0.3v(y_1) + 0.4v(y_2) + 0.3v(y_3)$$
$$= 7.08$$

The *ex post* utility function v leads us to the same ranking of *expected utility* as does the function u. Thus the *ex post* utility function is not unique, as would be the case with an absolute utility measure. However, it is not totally arbitrary either. Consider the *non-linear* transformation

$$v(y_i) = [u(y_i)]^2 \qquad \text{each } i$$

In this case the expected utility ranking changes because

$$V(L^1) = 0.2[u(50)]^2 + 0.6[u(25)]^2 + 0.2[u(10)]^2$$
$$= 0.416$$

while

$$V(L^2) = 0.3[u(50)]^2 + 0.4[u(25)]^2 + 0.3[u(10)]^2$$
$$= 0.444$$

giving L^2 a larger expected utility score! Thus arbitrary (non-linear) changes in u may change the rankings because of the change in utility ratios, but linear transformations are permissible. This result is often stated in the following form:

The (ex-post) utility measure is unique only up to a linear transformation.

This amounts to a degree of measurability (or *cardinality*) rather in the same way that we measure temperature. There is no absolute sense in which 20 ° Celsius is twice as warm as 10 °C since a linear transformation into Fahrenheit puts the higher temperature at about 1.36 times the lower (68 °F compared with 50 °F). (That the transformation of degrees Celcius into degrees Fahrenheit is linear is apparent from the equation $F = 32 + (9/5)C$ which is of the form $F = a + bC$.). Similarly we are no nearer to saying that in absolute terms one outcome gives twice the pleasure of another.

The scale of *ex post* utilities in this way generates a particular *ordering* of expected utilities which determines our choice. It is the ranking of *expected utilities* and not their absolute or even relative magnitude that matters, and *any* transformation linear or otherwise applied equally to our expected utilities will not change the ultimate ranking.

3.5 SOME PITFALLS WITH THE EXPECTED UTILITY HYPOTHESIS

The predictions of the expected utility hypothesis appear, so far, to accord with intuition and have led to apparently sensible choices between lotteries. It appears to offer a way of accounting for both the likelihood of events occurring and our feelings about taking chances with alternative lotteries. In short, it appears to offer a solution to the difficulties encountered in section 3.1.

However, the hypothesis stands or falls on the axioms, and we must be prepared to question the validity of the axioms if they generate unpalatable predictions or, equivalently perhaps, if a significant number of apparently reasonable people make choices which violate the hypothesis. Before presenting some examples it is worth outlining some general circumstances in which people may make choices that are inconsistent with this theory.

Firstly, behaviour may be affected by extremes. If the worst outcome is something really nasty, we may be unable to derive distinguishable standard prospects for each intermediate outcome. If we are reluctant to give any weight at all to y_4 in Axiom 3 whatever y_i we choose we will have $u_1 = 1$, $u_2 = 1$, $u_3 = 1$ and $u_4 = 0$ which makes the choice between any lotteries involving y_4 hard to establish (why?).

Secondly, despite Axiom 4, our choice between lotteries may depend on the way the alternatives are presented or on their *context*. Axiom 4 is sometimes known as the *independence axiom* and its violation results in paradoxical or inconsistent choices. There are many examples, one of the most famous being the *Allais Paradox*. Many experiments have reaffirmed the paradox and I consider a quite recent example, obtained from Kahneman and Tversky (1979).

Consider a choice between two lotteries L^1 and L^2 given by

$$L^1 = [(0.33, 2500), (0.66, 2400), (0.01, 0)]$$

$$L^2 = [(1, 2400)]$$

It does no harm to think of the outcomes as monetary gains (in pounds or dollars). Most respondents choose L^2 which implies

$$U(L^2) > U(L^1)$$

or $u(2400) > 0.33u(2500) + 0.66u(2400)$
or $0.34u(2400) > 0.33u(2500) \implies$

Now consider the choice between lotteries L^3 and L^4 given by

$$L^3 = [(0.33, 2500), (0.67, 0)]$$

$$L^4 = [(0.34, 2400), (0.66, 0)]$$

Most respondents choose L^3 implying

$$U(L^3) > U(L^4)$$

$$\text{or } 0.33u(2500) > 0.34u(2400)$$

which is inconsistent with the earlier revealed preference.

Of course, if individuals had forced themselves to take the consequences of the expected utility calculation, the choice of L^3 in the second choice problem would have been impossible. The message of this and other experiments is that people's judgement and feelings about risky choices are occasionally *not* independent of the context in which the choices appear. The expected utility hypothesis assumes that they are.

For most purposes the expected utility hypothesis is a satisfactory way of reaching decisions on risky choices even if occasionally our intuition is counter to it. The hypothesis is elegant, plausible and very convenient. We should, therefore, explore it a little further.

3.6 EXPECTED UTILITY AND ATTITUDES TO RISK

In the second example of section 3.3, I revealed a preference (in my choice of utility indices) for receiving 30 for certain rather than a fair lottery with an expected payoff of 30, and I attributed this preference to a dislike of taking chances. Put differently I displayed an aversion to taking a risk. While I believe most people would display a similar aversion it is not essential to the expected utility hypothesis that they do so and had I chosen my u_2 value differently in that case I might have displayed a willingness to take a chance on winning the largest outcome of 50.

Recall that the choice was between the lottery

$$L^3 = [(0.5, 50), (0.5, 10)]$$

and

$$L^4 = [(1.0, 30)]$$

I revealed that $U(L^4) > U(L^3)$ so that

$$u(30) > 0.5u(50) + 0.5u(10).$$

In other words the utility of the expected value of L^3, $u(30) = 0.70$, is greater than the expected utility of L^3. This is illustrated in Figure 3.1.

The utility function is initially composed of three points a, b, c associated with $u(10)$, $u(30)$ and $u(50)$ respectively. Suppose now we introduce

$$L^5 = [(1.0, 40)]$$

Clearly L^5 is going to be preferred to L^4 but how do we feel about L^5 and a lottery involving outcomes of 10 and 50 with the same

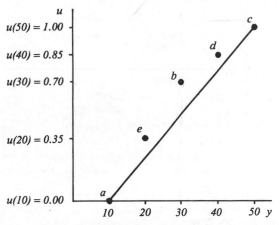

Figure 3.1: Ex post utility points

expected value? Clearly for such a lottery, say L^6, to have an expected value of 40 we must have

$$L^6 = [(0.75, 50), (0.25, 10)]$$

Things are clearly improving! But, am I yet prepared to sacrifice the certainty of 40 for a gamble with an expected payoff of 40? I think not. For me $u(40)$ is not going to be 0.75 but around 0.85. This gives another utility point d in Figure 3.1—that associated with $u(40)$, and thus

$$u(40) > 0.75u(50) + 0.25u(10).$$

What about a lottery involving 10 and 50 on the one hand and a certainty of 20? Well now, things do not look so good and a 10/50 lottery with an expected value of 20 now looks like,

$$L^7 = [(0.25, 50), (0.75, 10)]$$

However, 20 is still more than 10—the more likely outcome of the lottery. In other words, for me,

$$u(20) > 0.25u(50) + 0.75u(10)$$

Suppose $u(20) = 0.35$ and we have a fifth utility point e. We could continue with this procedure indefinitely choosing any conceivable money value for y and determining a utility value for it. The utility function would eventually have the smooth shape shown in Figure 3.2.

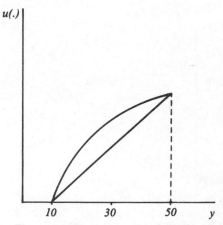

Figure 3.2: Smooth utility function

From now we will consider only smooth utility functions $u(y)$ defined over a specified range of values of y. However, the important thing is the shape of $u(y)$. Its concavity is a reflection of my *risk-averse* behaviour. Throughout, the utility derived from a particular y-value is *greater* than the expected utility from a lottery with the same expected money value. We can similarly define *risk-neutrality* as being where the utility of a particular y-value is *equal* to the expected utility from a lottery with the same value of y as its expected money reward. Risk-preferring behaviour is naturally, therefore, associated with a convex utility function.

Before finding a mathematical characterisation of these various attitudes to risk we summarize the result of this section so far.

An individual is risk-averse/neutral/-preferring if the utility of the expected outcome of a lottery exceeds/equals/is less than the expected utility of the lottery.

This discussion gives a clue as to a mathematical characterisation of attitudes to risk. Clearly, as long as the utility function is twice differentiable, as we will assume, the attitudes to risk are classified by the second derivative. Although $u'(y) > 0$ in each case we have $u'' < 0$ in the case of risk aversion, $u'' = 0$ in the case of risk neutrality and $u'' > 0$ in the case of risk-preference.

However, we would like to go further than this. It would be interesting to know whether there is any sense in the question: Which of two risk-averse individuals is the more risk-averse? It emerges that this is a sensible question and one with a ready answer.

Consult Figure 3.3 which shows the utility functions, u and v, of two individuals. Clearly $u(y)$ is more concave than $v(y)$ and intuitively we may associate greater risk-aversion with $u(y)$. However, we can show this more formally as follows. Let the expected value of a lottery be $\bar{y}$,

$$\bar{y} = py_{\max} + (1-p)y_{\min}$$

For individual u the utility of the expected value of the lottery $u(\bar{y})$ exceeds the expected utility of the lottery equal to $pu(y_{\max}) + (1-p)u(y_{\min}) = u(y_1)$—this of course reflects risk-aversion. Now suppose the expected value of the lottery is held constant at $\bar{y}$ but the amount available for certain as an alternative

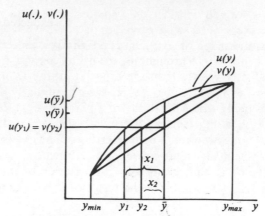

Figure 3.3: Concavity and risk premium

to the lottery is reduced by a small amount ε so that utility falls from $u(\bar{y})$ to $u(\bar{y} - \varepsilon)$. If ε is sufficiently small it is still the case that the certainty of receiving $\bar{y} - \varepsilon$ is preferred to the lottery with $\bar{y}$ as its expected outcome, that is, $u(\bar{y} - \varepsilon) > u(y_1)$. In fact, this will continue to be the case until an amount x_1 is deducted from the certain income which makes $u(\bar{y} - x_1) = u(y_1)$. Hence, x_1 is the largest amount that individual u is prepared to see eroded from the certain income and still prefer to avoid the gamble. The amount x_1 is known as the *risk-premium* for this individual under these circumstances, and obviously $x_1 = \bar{y} - y_1$.

Now suppose we do exactly the same for individual v. This individual's risk-premium satisfies $v(\bar{y} - x_2) = v(y_2)$, and $x_2 = \bar{y} - y_2$. We have,

$$x_1 = \bar{y} - y_1$$

and

$$x_2 = \bar{y} - y_2$$

but $y_2 > y_1$ and therefore $x_1 > x_2$. The more risk-averse individual has the higher risk-premium, is therefore prepared to give up more to avoid the risk and therefore places a greater value on the certainty.

By inspection of $u(y)$ and $v(y)$ it is clear that, at $\bar{y}$, u'' is more negative than v'' and so greater risk aversion is associated with greater concavity. Unfortunately we cannot simply take the second derivative as a measure of risk-aversion. We cannot simply say that it is more risk-averse than v because

$$- u'' > - v''$$

Although clearly true in Figure 3.3, remember we can always linearly transform u or v and therefore arbitrarily change the size of the second derivative at each y. For example, if we transform u according to

$$u_1(y) = a + bu(y) \qquad b > 1 \qquad (3.9)$$

then

$$u_1''(y) = bu''(y)$$

so that the individual is suddenly b times more risk-averse than before.

To overcome this we say that u is more risk-averse than v if $u'' < 0$, $v'' < 0$ and

$$\frac{- u''(y)}{u'(y)} > \frac{- v''(y)}{v'(y)} \qquad (3.10)$$

If this is true then a linear transformation of u according to (3.9) gives

$$\frac{- bu''(y)}{bu'(y)} = \frac{- u''(y)}{u'(y)} > \frac{- v''(y)}{v'(y)}$$

and (3.10) is preserved.

> For an individual with a utility function $u(y)$ the (Arrow–Pratt) measure of absolute risk-aversion is given by $R_A(y) = - u''(y)/u'(y)$

An individual is then risk-averse if $R_A(y)$ is positive, risk-neutral if $R_A(y)$ is zero and risk-perferring if $R_A(y)$ is negative. A person is more risk-averse the larger is $R_A(y)$.

A disadvantage with $R_A(y)$ is that its value depends on the units chosen for y in general. Consider the following example. The utility function is given by

$$u(y) = \ln(y) \qquad y > 0$$

so that

$$u'(y) = \frac{1}{y} > 0$$

and

$$u''(y) = \frac{-1}{y^2} < 0$$

Hence,

$$R_A(y) = \frac{1}{y}$$

If y is measured in pounds sterling $R_A(y) = 1$, if measured in pence $R_A(y) = 0.01$. It would be preferable if a measure of risk-aversion took the form of a pure number, such as an elasticity. Happily this is achieved by the (Arrow–Pratt) measure of relative risk-aversion.

$$R_R(y) = -y\frac{u''(y)}{u'(y)} = yR_A$$

In the above example $R_R(y) = 1$ regardless of y's units.

That $R_A(y)$ and $R_R(y)$ depend on y is an indicator that they are *local* measures of risk aversion. To see the importance of this we return to Figure 3.2 and reinterpret the value $y = 30$ as an amount already in our possession and we are given the opportunity of playing a game in which we face a 50–50 chance of gaining or losing 20. A risk-averter will turn down this opportunity and keep the 30, and the risk-premium shows how much the individual will pay to avoid the gamble (Figure 3.3). Suppose we start with an amount greater than 30; are we more or less likely to avoid the gamble of gaining or losing 20? If we suppose we had a wealth of 1,000 already in our possession, then a gamble involving the possible loss of 20 surely involves less of a threat! This effect is summarized as follows.

> A risk-averter who fears fair gambles less when wealth is greater has a utility function which exhibits decreasing absolute risk-aversion

that is, $R_A(y) < 0$.

Although not a universal rule, many people appear to exhibit decreasing risk-aversion with increased wealth. The fact that an individual degree of risk-aversion may vary with y justifies our notation of $R_A(y)$.

3.7   CONCLUSION

We have travelled far enough along this road. An opportunity to practise the lessons of this chapter may be found in the exercises. Further issues and developments may be found later in the book and in the bibliographic sources. For now, I would like to tie up some loose ends.

All of the lotteries discussed here have involved money rewards. The theory does not require this. However, we must feel happy about ranking mixtures of money and non-money outcomes (Axiom 1). The generality of the theory in this case depends on our ability to say such things as:

$$50 \gtrsim 40 \gtrsim \text{ being interviewed on television.}$$

In the remainder of this book at least ultimate outcomes will be in money terms or (cheating slightly) money equivalents.

Finally, our derivation of the hypothesis was in terms of a discrete number of outcomes and an associated (discrete) probability distribution. The last section introduced the idea that utility functions may be continuous on a specified interval of ys. The implication is that the accompanying probability distribution is also continuous. In this case expected utility over the interval is given by

$$U = \int_{y_{min}}^{u_{max}} yf(y) \, \mathrm{d}y$$

where $f(y)$ is the probability density function of ys.

3.8 BIBLIOGRAPHIC GUIDE

Alternative treatments of the expected utility hypothesis are to be found in most good graduate microeconomic texts including Deaton and Muellbauer (1980), Gravelle and Rees (1981), Green (1971), Layard and Walters (1978). A more general treatment is to be found in Hey (1979). The hypothesis is due largely to von Neuman and Morgenstern (1944) especially Ch. 3 and Appendix, though most modern proofs are based on Luce and Raiffa (1957).

The Allais Paradox is discussed in Savage (1954) as well as Allais (1953)

Alternatives to the expected utility approach have been suggested by Kahneman and Tversky (1979) and Loomes and Sugden (1982). More fundamental criticisms have been made by Simon (1959) and Shackle, summarized in Ford (1983).

Measures of risk-aversion were developed by Arrow (1965) and Pratt (1964). Hey (1979) provides an obvious sequel to the material covered here.

3.9 EXERCISES

3.1 Examine the affect on my ordering of lotteries L^3 and L^4 in section 3.3 of choosing (i) $u_2 = 0.5$, (ii) $u_2 = 0.4$. What is being revealed about my preferences in each case?

3.2 Consider the following possible outcomes.

$$y_1 = 100 \qquad y_2 = 10 \qquad y_3 = -4 \qquad y_4 = \text{execution}$$

How do you rank the following lotteries according to the expected utility hypothesis?

$$L^1 = [(0.1, 100), (0.3, 10), (0.4, -4), (0.1, \text{execution})]$$
$$L^2 = [(0.2, 100), (0.2, 10), (0.4, -4), (0.2, \text{execution})]$$

(You are required to take the threat of execution seriously!)

3.3 An individual is offered a choice between

$$L^1 = [(0.8, 4000), (0.2, 0)]$$
$$L^2 = [(1.0, 3000)]$$

and chooses L^2. Which of the following will the same individual choose according to the expected utility hypothesis?

$$L^3 = [(0.2, 4000), (0.8, 0)]$$
$$L^4 = [(0.25, 3000, (0.75, 0)]$$

Is this what you would expect?

3.4 Consider the ordering of expected utilities associated with the choice between L^1 and L^2 in section 3.3. Show that functions $V(L^1)$ and $V(L^2)$ produce the same ordering where

$$V(L^i) = z_1^{p_1^i} z_2^{p_2^i} z_3^{p_3^i} \qquad i = 1, 2$$

3.5 This chapter asserted a principle of decreasing absolute risk-aversion. What principle would you assert for relative risk-aversions as income increases?

3.6 Suppose the (*ex post*) utility function of an individual takes the (quadratic) form

$$u(y) = a + by - \tfrac{1}{2}y^2 \qquad y < b$$

What attitudes to risk are implied by this function. Is this behaviour reasonable?

3.7 (a) Suppose the utility function takes the form

$$u(y) = a - be^{-ry} \qquad r \neq 0$$

What is the absolute measure of risk-aversion in this case?

(b) What is $R_A(y)$ if the utility function takes the form,

$$u(y) = a - by^{-r+1} \qquad r \neq 1$$

What is $R_R(y)$ in this case?

3.8 What attitude to risk is displayed by the utility function

$$u(y) = \ln(y) \qquad y > 0$$

Is this behaviour reasonable?

4. The Theory of the Firm Under Uncertainty

4.1 INTRODUCTION

This is one of the oldest branches of economic analysis under uncertainty. However, I choose to examine it now, at such an early stage in the book, not for this reason but because it is a useful vehicle with which to demonstrate some of the calculus of expected utility theory. More importantly, even within the context of very simple models, it is possible to see the difference the introduction of uncertainty makes to familiar theories. These differences fall into two main types. Firstly there is the impact of uncertainty on the market environment. This involves thinking carefully about how uncertainty is to be introduced (which factors are to be 'uncertain') and about how the structure of the model is to be built. Secondly there is the impact of uncertainty on the comparative-static properties of the model.

Firms face very different market environments both as suppliers of goods and as demanders of factors of production, and any or all of these markets may present the firm with a variety of uncertainties. Furthermore, with complex organisations and production processes there may be many sources of uncertainty from *within* the firm. In principle, we could rewrite here the whole of the 'theory of the firm' to account for 'uncertainty', but I choose a different path. In sections 4.2 and 4.3 I present two models of the equivalent of a 'perfectly competitive' firm under uncertainty. In the first, uncertainty arises in the production process, while in the second the firm is uncertain as to the market price for its output. In section 4.4, I examine some issues arising out of the theory of monopoly under uncertainty and in sections 4.5 and 4.6 I suggest that inventories are a natural response by firms to demand uncertainty.

4.2 THE PRICE-TAKER AND PRODUCTION UNCERTAINTY

Recall from Chapter 1 our discussion of 'perfectly competitive' markets under uncertainty. In the conventional microeconomic analysis 'perfect information' is a key assumption of the perfect competition model, and this severely limits the ways in which uncertainty enters the picture without destroying the 'price-taking' nature of perfectly competitive firms. In this section and the following one I introduce uncertainty in two ways which preserve or do not logically contradict the 'price-taker' assumption. Later, at the beginning of section 4.4, assumptions are suggested which run counter to the nature of price-taking behaviour.

By a price-taker I mean a firm which takes the price of its product and the wages of its workforce as given by the goods and labour markets respectively. The firm is sufficiently unimportant to ignore the effect of its decisions on market conditions.

The firm's objective is to maximise the expected utility of profit, $U(\pi)$ where the *ex post* utility of a profit level is (using the notation of the last chapter) $u(\pi)$. In this section the firm faces production uncertainty and I propose to model this in the following way.

Output is determined as usual by the short-run production function

$$x = x(l) \qquad (4.1)$$

where x is output, l is the labour input (suitably measured) and $x'(l) > 0$ (positive marginal product), $x''(l) < 0$ (diminishing marginal product). However, I assume that production may be intercepted, say by the breakdown of a crucial piece of equipment. For simplicity, the breakdown, if it occurs, results in no output forthcoming, and output $x(l)$ is produced otherwise. If q is the probability that no breakdown occurs and $(1 - q)$ is the probability of breakdown then realised profit takes one of two values:

$$\pi_1 = px(l) - wl - a \qquad \text{with probability } q$$

$$\pi_2 = -wl - a \qquad \text{with probability } (1 - q) \qquad (4.2)$$

where p is the (given) product price, w is the (given) wage rate and a is a fixed cost of production. In (4.2) the assumption is that the firm incurs all existing costs when production is intercepted.

Expected utility is, therefore,

$$U(\pi) = qu(\pi_1) + (1 - q)u(\pi_2) \qquad \pi_2 < \pi_1 \qquad (4.3)$$

The firm under these circumstances has no control over p, w or a and only partial control over x, and therefore its only choice is l. The firm chooses l so as to maximise (4.3). The first-order condition is

$$qu'(\pi_1)(px'(l) - w) - (1 - q)u'(\pi_2)w = 0 \qquad (4.4)$$

which solves to give

$$\frac{w}{p} = x'(l^*)\left\{ \frac{qu'(\pi_1^*)}{qu'(\pi_1^*) + (1 - q)u'(\pi_2^*)} \right\} \qquad (4.5)$$

where $u'(\pi_i^*)$ means $u'(\pi_i)$ evaluated at l^*—the solution to (4.4). It is easy to establish that under certainty (i.e. $q = 1$) the solution to (4.4) is $\hat{l}$ given by

$$\frac{w}{p} = x'(\hat{l}) \qquad (4.6)$$

which is familiar equality between the real wage and the marginal product of labour of competitive analysis. So, how does l^*, the level of employment under uncertainty, differ from $\hat{l}$, the level of employment under certainty? At $q = 1$ there is no difference between l^* and $\hat{l}$, but we may use (4.4) to investigate how l^* changes as q changes. Applying the implicit function theorem to (4.4) gives,

$$\frac{dl^*}{dq} = \frac{-\{u'(\pi_1)px'(l) + [u'(\pi_2) - u'(\pi_1)]w\}}{\{qu''\pi_1[px'(l) - w]^2 + qu'(\pi_1)px''(l) + (1 - q)u''(\pi_2)w^2\}} \qquad (4.7)$$

I will assume that the firm is risk-averse in which case since $\pi_2 < \pi_1$, $u'(\pi_2) > u'(\pi_1)$ and so the numerator is negative. The denominator is also negative, being the second-order condition of the maximum. Hence, as q falls l^* also falls. If $l^* = \hat{l}$ for $q = 1$, then $l^* < \hat{l}$ for $q < 1$.

> The risk-averse price-taker has lower employment under production uncertainty than a price-taker with certain production.

Interestingly the *risk-neutral* price-taker also has a lower employ-

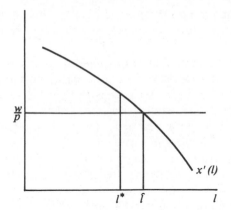

Figure 4.1: Employment under production uncertainty

ment than the certain price-taker! The reason is that even with risk-neutrality there is still some concavity in the utility function through concavity of $x(l)$. The firm's valuation of the profitability of a particular employment level in this case owes as much to diminishing marginal productivity as it does to risk-aversion. The verification of this result is left as an exercise.

It is a corollary of this analysis that under production uncertainty labour is paid *less* than its marginal contribution to output—the braced term in (4.5) is a positive fraction—unlike the certainty case given by (4.6). The position is illustrated in Figure 4.1. Clearly in this model the demand for labour is not given by the marginal product curve.

4.3   THE PRICE—TAKER AND MARKET PRICE UNCERTAINTY

This problem is one of the most thoroughly explored in the literature. The firm is to be thought of as the helpless victim of uncertainty in the market. The only complication to the conventional competition model is that rather than facing a known market price, the firm faces many possible prices distributed according to the known probability density, $f(p)$. As with the previous model the firm must take its decision before the state of the world is known, in this case before the market price is known for certain.

However, in this model the firm is able to choose its output, x, directly and once more maximises the expected utility of profit written this time as

$$U(\pi) = \int u(px - c(x) - a)f(p)\,\mathrm{d}p \qquad (4.8)$$

We will assume, in conformity with standard analysis, that variable costs, $c(x)$ increase with output ($c'(x) > 0$). Integration in (4.8) and throughout this section is over all positive values of p. Notice that one crucial assumption may be carried over from the certainty case without much difficulty; whatever the market price turns out to be, the firm will be able to sell all of its output.

The first-order condition for the choice of x maximising (4.8) is,

$$\int u'(\pi)[p - c'(x)]f(p)\,\mathrm{d}p = 0 \qquad (4.9)$$

Contrast this with the certainty case in which the *known* market price is given by $\bar{p}$, the mean price under uncertainty. We have the familiar condition that

$$\bar{p} - c'(x) = 0 \qquad (4.10)$$

which of course gives the 'price equals marginal cost' condition. How does the solution to the uncertainty case, say x^*, differ from the solution to the certainty case (4.10), say $\hat{x}$? First consider the respective second-order conditions. Under certainty we have (from (4.10)).

$$-c''(\hat{x}) < 0 \qquad (4.11)$$

which requires increasing marginal cost ($c''(x) > 0$), while under uncertainty we have (from (4.9))

$$\int u''(\pi^*)[p - c'(x^*)]^2 f(p)\,\mathrm{d}p - c''(x^*)\int u''(\pi^*)f(p)\,\mathrm{d}p < 0 \qquad (4.12)$$

(where π^* means 'π evaluated at $x = x^*$').

Clearly, we do not need $c''(x) > 0$ for (4.12) to hold. This is the first difference—x^* *may* be chosen in a zone of decreasing marginal cost. This would *never* be optimal under certainty.

To see how x^* stands in relation to $\hat{x}$ consider (4.9) and rewrite this as

$$\int u'(\pi^*)pf(p)\,\mathrm{d}p = c'(x^*)\int u'(\pi^*)f(p)\,\mathrm{d}p$$

or

$$c'(x^*) = \int u'(\pi^*)pf(p)\,\mathrm{d}p \Big/ \int u'(\pi^*)f(p)\,\mathrm{d}p \qquad (4.13)$$

and compare this with (from 4.10)

$$c'(\hat{x}) = \bar{p} \equiv \int pf(p)\,\mathrm{d}p \qquad (4.14)$$

Now, assuming identical cost conditions under uncertainty and under certainty, the left-hand side of (4.13) and that of (4.14) are equal at $x^* = \hat{x}$. Given that $\hat{x}$ must be in a zone of increasing marginal cost, $x^* < \hat{x}$ if $c'(x^*) < c'(\hat{x})$. Hence $x^* < \hat{x}$ if

$$\int pf(p)\,\mathrm{d}p > \int u'(\pi^*)pf(p)\,\mathrm{d}p \Big/ \int u'(\pi^*)f(p)\,\mathrm{d}p \qquad (4.15)$$

That this is indeed the case is shown by a simple proof which some readers might prefer to skip.

Note that (4.15) may be rewritten,

$$0 > \int u'(\pi^*)(p - \bar{p})f(p)\,\mathrm{d}p \qquad (4.16)$$

From the definition of profit, π differs from its expected value $\bar{\pi}$ only to the extent that revenue px^* differs from its expected value $\bar{p}x^*$. Furthermore, $\pi = \bar{\pi}$ if $p = \bar{p}$, $\pi > \bar{\pi}$ if $p > \bar{p}$ and $\pi < \bar{\pi}$ if $p < \bar{p}$. I will assume that the firm is risk-averse, that is, $u''(\pi) < 0$, from which it follows that $u'(\pi) < u'(\bar{\pi})$ if $p > \bar{p}$ and $u'(\pi) > u'(\bar{\pi})$ if $p < \bar{p}$. For reasons which will become clear, I am interested in the behaviour of the quantity

$$\lambda(p) \equiv [u'(\bar{\pi}) - u'(\pi)](p - \bar{p}) \qquad (4.17)$$

at various values of p. At $p = \bar{p}$, $\lambda(p) = 0$, and differentiating $\lambda(p)$ (noting that $\bar{p}$ is a constant and $u''(\pi) < 0$) gives,

$$\lambda'(p) = -u''(\pi)x^*(p - \bar{p}) + [u'(\bar{\pi}) - u'(\pi)]$$

$\lessgtr 0$ depending as $p \lessgtr \bar{p}$

The graph of $\lambda(p)$ is shown in Figure 4.2.

It follows that $\lambda(p)$ is positive (except at $p = \bar{p}$ where it is zero) and

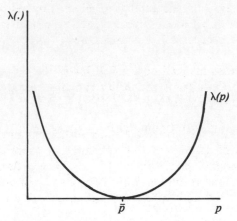

Figure 4.2: Behaviour of equation (4.17)

so,

$$u'(\bar{\pi})(p - \bar{p}) > u'(\pi)(p - \bar{p}) \qquad p \neq \bar{p}$$

Taking expectations of both sides gives,

$$u'(\bar{\pi}) \int (p - \bar{p}) f(p) \, \mathrm{d}p > \int u'(\pi)(p - \bar{p}) f(p) \, \mathrm{d}p$$

but,

$$\int (p - \bar{p}) f(p) \, \mathrm{d}p = \int p f(p) \, \mathrm{d}p - \bar{p} = 0$$

Hence,

$$0 > \int u'(\pi)(p - \bar{p}) f(p) \, \mathrm{d}p$$

establishing (4.16).

> The risk-averse price-taker facing price uncertainty produces a lower output than the perfectly competitive firm under certainty facing the same mean price.

We write, 'facing the same mean price' because we have compared the choice of x^* with that made when facing a certain price of $\bar{p}$.

The corollary, using (4.13) and (4.14), is that the firm under uncertainty chooses an output at a point where marginal cost is less than the mean price.

Further analysis of this general problem is outside the scope of this book but one further property of the model is stated here without proof because of its great interest.

An increase in fixed cost a will lower the output of a risk-averse price-taker if the utility function displays decreasing absolute risk-aversion.

This is in contrast to the result under certainty known to all first-year students of economics that a change in fixed cost does not affect the marginal condition (4.10) and hence does not affect output. Under uncertainty an increase in fixed cost does not affect marginal cost but does affect the marginal utility evaluation of profit.

4.4   THE UNCERTAIN MONOPOLIST

The role of the competitive firm as a quantity-setting price-taker was not affected by the introduction of uncertainty. A firm could still sell all of its output at whatever price eventually emerged in the market. In practice firms are not assured of this and in the theory of the firm under uncertainty it is the downward-sloping product demand curve which causes the difficulty. Under certainty, the monopolist may sell all available output as long as the price given by the demand curve is accepted. Under uncertainty where decisions are made on the basis of expectations there is scope for actual sales to differ from output. In this section some implications of this for the modelling of the monopoly problem are considered. The following two sections look at the implications for an explicit modelling of inventories.

Before attempting a general discussion of modelling the uncertain monopolist I shall present a simple model of price determination under monopoly. Recall from standard textbooks that a monopolist may set price *or* output but not both. A price-setting monopolist takes the output required from the demand curve and all of the resulting output is demanded. Denote by $Q(p)$ the demand for a monopolist's output at price p. We have that $Q'(p) < 0$ (less is demanded at a higher price). Under certainty the problem is to choose price so as to maximise profit

$$\pi = pQ(p) - c[Q(p)] - a \qquad (4.18)$$

where $c(.)$ is the variable cost function and a the fixed cost. To keep things simple suppose that the cost function takes a cubic form $c[Q(p)] = [Q(p)]^3$. The first-order condition for the maximisation of (4.18) by choice of p is (using the cubic cost function)

$$Q(\hat{p}) + \hat{p}Q'(\hat{p}) - 3[Q(\hat{p})]^2 Q'(\hat{p}) = 0 \qquad (4.19)$$

where $\hat{p}$ is the profit-maximising choice of price under certainty.

The modelling of uncertainty can be very involved in these models and I will keep things as simple as possible here. Uncertainty will enter into the demand curve in the following way. Demand will fluctuate randomly about the 'certain' demand curve $Q(p)$ so that *ex post* realised demand will be $Q(p)$ plus or minus a random 'error' term $Q(p) + \varepsilon$, $\varepsilon \gtreqless 0$. I will assume that ε has a zero mean so that expected demand at price p is given by

$$\int [Q(p) + \varepsilon] f(\varepsilon)\, d\varepsilon = Q(p) \qquad (4.20)$$

In fact, I will suppose that ε has a *uniform* distribution between -1 and $+1$;

$$f(\varepsilon) = \begin{cases} \tfrac{1}{2} & -1 \leqslant \varepsilon \leqslant 1 \\ 0 & \text{otherwise} \end{cases} \qquad (4.21)$$

Keeping the problem as simple as possible I assume that the firm faces a linear (inverse) demand curve so that $Q''(p) = 0$.

Finally, I assume that the firm maximises expected *profit* rather than expected utility of profit. This last assumption is equivalent in its implications to risk-neutrality. Given our assumptions expected profit is given by

$$\bar{\pi} = \tfrac{1}{2} \int_{-1}^{+1} \{p[Q(p) + \varepsilon] - [Q(p) + \varepsilon]^3 - a\}\, d\varepsilon \qquad (4.22)$$

The first-order condition is (after evaluating the integral terms in ε),

$$Q(p^*) + p^* Q'(p^*) - 3[Q(p^*)]^2 Q'(p^*) - 2Q'(p^*) = 0 \qquad (4.23)$$

Denote the left-hand side of (4.19) by $\lambda(\hat{p})$, then (4.19) and (4.23) may be written,

$$\lambda(\hat{p}) = 0 \qquad (4.19)'$$

$$\lambda(p^*) - 2Q'(p^*) = 0 \qquad (4.23)'$$

The second-order condition in each case implies $\lambda'(p) < 0$. Now, since $Q'(p)$ is negative it follows that $\lambda(p^*) < \lambda(\hat{p})$, which in turn implies that $p^* > \hat{p}$. Thus, even with this very simple example, using very restrictive assumptions we have produced an example of uncertainty in demand raising the monopoly price.

Unfortunately, this result is by no means general and although some of our assumptions were used purely for simplification (uniform distribution and additivity of the random term) in more general models it is the interplay between risk-aversion and the cost function which is crucial. In our simple example above, the absence of risk-aversion means that all the concavity in profit required to produce different behaviour under uncertainty must be provided by the cost function.

Our illustration used the example of an uncertain monopolist choosing price. We could, on the other hand, have the monopolist choosing quantity in the face of the demand curve $p(Q)$, in which case a slight change of notation gives profit as

$$\pi = p(Q)Q - c(Q) - a \qquad (4.24)$$

Randomness may enter into demand and a similar analysis may be conducted as for the price-setting except, of course, this time q, is chosen.

Under certainty, price-setting and quantity-setting are the only two alternatives for the monopolist and they are mutually exclusive. Under uncertainty this is not the case. Think of the price-setting monopolist again. As things stand the output will be uncertain *ex ante* and will eventually meet *ex post* demand. This is unreasonable as a description of production on an uncertain environment. Under uncertainty a price may be set but will have associated with it a whole distribution of possible demands. Typically, firms must be ready with output available to meet eventual demand and this requires a pre-commitment to a level of output, x. *Ex post*, the firm may sell no more than x and may sell less than x if demand is less than output. Sales are therefore given by the smaller of *output*, x, and *demand*, Q. Thus, under uncertainty both price *and* output may be predetermined but ultimate sales (and hence profit) are determined by demand if $Q < x$ and only by output if $x < Q$.

I do not propose to go into this problem formally here but it is useful to give some further thought to an important implication of the output–demand–sales distinction. If demand falls short of output in some periods and exceeds output in others it will make sense for a firm to *plan* to hold stocks of its goods. An *inventory* provides a 'use' for unsold output and a resource with which to satisfy excess demand.

4.5　INVENTORY DECISIONS

The models considered so far have been single-period models and an implicit assumption has been made that the good produced is *perishable* and may not be stored for future sales. Indeed in these models the 'future' does not exist—only the 'present'. Notice, for example, that in the last section we did not explore the consequences of demand falling short of that expected because there were no consequences following on from this event in the future. In this section I will outline some issues surrounding the modelling of inventories in the context of a very simple model based on a two-period extension of the price-taker facing price uncertainty. However, to keep the problem as simple as possible I make some modifications to the earlier model of section 4.3.

The firm faces a two-period life in which it chooses output in each period, x_1 and x_2, and an inventory, y, to be carried over into the second period. Output is chosen in each period prior to the realisation of prices and the inventory decision is taken at the same time as the decision on x_1—the beginning of the first period. In the second period, expected profit when x_2 is produced, y is carried over from the previous period and expected price is $\bar{p}$ is given by

$$\pi_2(x_2, y) = (x_2 + y)\bar{p}_2 - c(x_2) - m(y) \qquad (4.25)$$

where $(c(x_2)$ is the cost of production, $c'(x_2) > 0$, $c''(x_2) > 0$ and $m(y)$ the cost of holding the inventory, $m'(y) > 0$, $m''(y) > 0)$. The first term in (4.25) is second-period expected revenue. Clearly x_2^* satisfies

$$\bar{p}_2 = c'(x_2^*) \qquad (4.26)$$

At the beginning of the first period the entire expected profit is

$$\pi(x_1, y) = \bar{p}_1(x_1 - y) - c(x_1) + (x_2^* + y)\bar{p}_2 - c(x_2^*) - m(y) \tag{4.27}$$

which has an obvious interpretation. For a given y, x_1 is chosen so that

$$\bar{p}_1 = c'(x_1^*) \tag{4.28}$$

Notice that the *cost functions* are assumed to be the same in each period, that $\bar{p}_1$ does not necessarily equal $\bar{p}_2$ and that $\bar{p}_2$ is unaffected by any event in the first period—in particular $\bar{p}_2$ is independent of the realised value of first-period price. Now, given that x_1 and x_2 are determined (by 4.27 and 4.28) and that any amount may be sold at the prevailing market price, is there any advantage to *this* firm of holding stock between periods?

The cost of holding back one unit of output as inventory is the lost revenue in the first period plus the marginal cost of holding the inventory, $\bar{p}_1 + m'$. The gain to the firm is the extra revenue generated in period two, $\bar{p}_2$. As long as $\bar{p}_2 > \bar{p}_1 + m'$ it pays the firm to hold an inventory. By doing so it looses first-period revenue, of course, but is able to supply $x_2 + y$ to the market at a lower cost than producing all of $x_2 + y$ in the second period. Choosing y in (4.27) gives, as the intuitive argument suggests

$$\bar{p}_2 = \bar{p}_1 + m'(y^*) \tag{4.29}$$

Thus a necessary condition for optimal inventory holding is $\bar{p}_2 > \bar{p}_1$. Figure 4.3 illustrates the position. Output x_1 is determined by (4.28) and x_2 by (4.26)—the diagram assumes $\bar{p}_2 > \bar{p}_1$. Notice that the marginal cost of supplying $(x_2 + y)$ from inventories is equal to $\bar{p}_2$ and is lower than the marginal cost of producing the whole of $(x_2 + y)$ in period two for any value of y, Clearly the level of the optimal inventory depends on the gap between $\bar{p}_2$ and $\bar{p}_1$.

If the second-period receipts are discounted by a factor $\rho \equiv 1/(1 + r)$ (a higher time-preference rate r causing a lower weight to be attached to second-period profit), (4.27) becomes (assuming that inventory costs are incurred in the second period)

$$\pi(x_1, y) = \bar{p}_1(x_1 - y) - c(x_1) + \rho\{\bar{p}_2(x_2^* - y) - c(x_2^*) - m(y)\} \tag{4.30}$$

and (4.29) becomes

$$\bar{p}_1 = \rho[\bar{p}_2 - m'(y)] > 0 \tag{4.31}$$

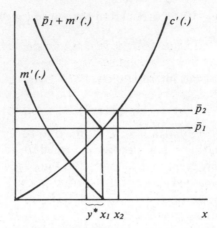

Figure 4.3: Inventory holding and expected price increase

in which case inventory holding is only optimal if $\bar{p}_1 < \rho\bar{p}_2$. Using
(4.31) it is apparent that the optimal inventory increases with ρ and
$\bar{p}_2$ and falls with $\bar{p}_1$. Verification of these results is left as an
exercise. An increase in $\bar{p}_2$ raises the present value of expected profit in the second period, as does an increase in ρ, hence, the firm
holds back more of its first-period output to be released on to the
market in the following period.

Notice that this is a very 'partial' view of the workings of the
market. If all firms expect higher prices then everyone will
recognise that the market will be flooded next period and the
expected price increase will not materialise. To keep things simple
I have abstracted from the problems of market equilibrium and
expectation formation. Even so the results are suggestive and the
role played by the discount factor is similar to that of more complicated models.

4.6   FURTHER ANALYSIS OF INVENTORIES

The model of the previous section proposed that inventories may
be held if prices are expected to rise. There are other responses to
this type of price uncertainty and these are discussed in Chapter 6.
For now, we consider a different model of inventory which appears
frequently in the literature. The model, which does not consider

production explicitly, is sometimes known as the *retailers' problem*.

A retail store specialising in the sale of a single, perfectly divisible commodity, buys from a wholesaler at a known price c per unit and sells to the consumer at the known, certain price p. At the beginning of the period the shop contains x items and further items may be ordered, with immediate delivery for sale during the period. We consider only the one-period problem. The total inventory for the period, y, is the sum of items already in stock, x, and the items ordered.

Uncertainty enters this model because the demand forthcoming from shoppers is random, and the inventory must be established before the period's demand Q is realised. In addition to the re-ordering cost of c per unit, the retailer incurs a holding cost of k per unit if realised demand falls short of the total stock available and a cost of s per unit of unsatisfied demand. If demand has a distribution with the continuous density $f(Q)$ then total expected costs when the store orders $(y - x)$ items is given by,

$$C(x, y) = c[y - x] + k \int_0^y (y - Q)f(Q)\,dQ$$

$$+ s \int_y^\infty (Q - y)f(Q)\,dQ \qquad (4.32)$$

where the first term on the right-hand side of (4.32) is the total re-ordering cost, the second term is the total expected holding cost and the final term is the total expected sales penalty. Total expected revenue on the other hand is,

$$R(y) = p \int_0^y Qf(Q)\,dQ + py \int_y^\infty f(Q)\,dQ \qquad (4.33)$$

where the first term on the right-hand side of (4.33) is the expected total revenue when demand falls short of the total stock y and the second term is the total expected revenue when demand exceeds y, in this case py is received—an event with probability

$$\int_y^\infty f(Q)\,dQ = [1 - F(y)] \qquad (4.34)$$

where $F(y)$ is the cumulative distribution associated with $f(.)$.

The retailer is assumed to be an expected profit-maximiser where profit is obviously given by

$$\pi(x, y) = R(y) - C(x, y) \qquad (4.35)$$

Since x is given at the start of the period the retailer's problem is to choose the level of inventory y and hence how much, if anything, is to be ordered, $x - y$. It is readily shown that the solution to this problem implies that the optimal inventory, y^*, satisfies;

$$F(y^*) = \frac{(p + s - c)}{(p + s + k)} \qquad (4.36)$$

which requires $c < p + s$, since $F(y^*)$ must be a positive fraction. The optimal stock level is given by (4.36) but the implied reordering policy depends on the size of y^* relative to x, the beginning of period stock. Clearly if $y^* > x$ the profit-maximising stock level implies an order for $y^* - x$ items, whereas if $y^* = x$ the optimum policy is to order nothing—that is, (4.35) attains its maximum at $y = x$. However, in a stable environment in which p, s, c, k and $F(.)$ are constant over time, and if when the retailer started x was zero, the retailer should never face the position in which $y^* = x$ (why?). Changes in the parameters will generally change y^* and in those periods it may be the case that the optimal stock is less than the beginning-of-period holding.

This concludes our analysis of inventories. Further analyses are referred to in the Bibliographic guide and some further results are left as exercises.

4.7   CONCLUSION

I have examined a variety of topics in the theory of the firm under uncertainty but many more topics have been ignored or only touched upon.

One important area not examined here is that of the oligopoly market form. This interesting area can be very complex. Not only does uncertainty enter into the analysis as alternative states of nature, but interdependence between producers often alluded to in micro texts gives scope for strategic play. The theory of games, therefore, plays an important role in this area including that of providing many of the equilibrium concepts.

4.8 BIBLIOGRAPHIC GUIDE

Very simply, I refer the reader to Hey (1979) for an elaboration and generalisation of many of the models of this chapter. In addition the inventory problem is given a fuller, more rigorous treatment in Hey (1981) and DeGroot (1970).

4.9 EXERCISES

4.1 Prove the claim made in the text that, in the context of the model of section 4.2, a risk-neutral firm facing the threat of interrupted production will have a lower employment level than if production were certain.

4.2 Using the inventory model discussed around equation (4.30), establish the claims in the text that an increase in ρ and $\bar{p}_2$, and a fall in $\bar{p}_1$ all have the effect of increasing the inventory.

4.3 In the one-period retailer's problem of section 4.6, examine the effect on the optimal inventory y of increases in the unit ordering cost, c, and the unit holding cost, k.

4.4 Again using the retailer's problem of section 4.6, suppose that in addition to the unit re-ordering cost of c per item there is a fixed cost, a, imposed by the wholesaler for each order. Set up and solve the retailer's problem in this case. What is the optimal re-ordering policy?

5. Consumption and Saving

5.1 INTRODUCTION

The idea of an inventory introduced in the last chapter was based on the notion that a producer may hold stocks of a non-perishable good either to exploit expected improvements in market conditions or, more generally, to provide a hedge against further uncertainties. Similar possibilities clearly exist for individual consumers. Income to be received in future periods may be uncertain and income which is received may be disposed of in a variety of ways. We examine problems of this type in this chapter. In the following section a simple two-period consumption–saving model is presented in which uncertainty about second-period income plays a part in determining the amount of first-period income to be carried over into the second period as savings. In section 5.3 further analysis of the two-period problem examines the role of interest rate uncertainty in determining savings. In both of these sections the choice is simply one between consumption and saving. The way in which savings may be carried over from one period to the next—the problem of *portfolio choice*—is the subject of section 5.4. The way in which income is spent in consumption—a traditional concern of microeconomic texts—is not discussed here.

5.2 SAVINGS AND INCOME UNCERTAINTY

Consider an individual facing the problem of deciding how much of today's income to consume and how much to save until tomorrow. In general, we may think of such an individual having a utility function which depends on consumption 'today', c_1, and consumption 'tomorrow', c_2, denoted by

$$U(c_1, c_2) \qquad (5.1)$$

However, suppose that tomorrow's consumption opportunities

58

depend not only on the proportion of today's income carried over, but also on the receipt of a hitherto uncertain income. Clearly in these circumstances tomorrow's consumption c_2 may not be chosen directly. If y_1 is today's (known) income, y_2 is tomorrow's (as yet unknown) income and i is interest earned on savings, then the total amount available for consumption tomorrow will be

$$(y_1 - c_1)(1 + i) + y_2 \qquad (5.2)$$

and we assume that the individual does in fact consume all of the funds available. Hence, denoting the rate of return $(1 + i)$ by ρ we have,

$$c_2 = \rho(y_1 - c_1) + y_2 \qquad (5.3)$$

However, at the time the savings decision (the first-period consumption decision) is made y_2 is a random variable. For simplicity suppose that second-period income takes the value 0 with probability p and $y_2 \ (> 0)$ with probability $(1 - p)$ then we have

$$c_2 = \begin{cases} c_2(0) \equiv \rho(y_1 - c_1) & \text{with probability } p \\ c_2(y_2) \equiv \rho(y_1 - c_1) + y_2 & \text{with probability } (1 - p) \end{cases} \qquad (5.4)$$

Since $y_2 > 0$, then $c_2(y_2) > c_2(0)$. Finally, suppose that the total expected utility (5.1) takes the form

$$U(c_1, c_2) = u(c_1) + \{pu(c_2(0)) + (1 - p)u(c_2(y_2))\} \qquad (5.5)$$

That is, total (expected) utility is the sum of the first-period (certain) utility (the first term on the right-hand side of (5.5) and the second-period expected utility (given by the braced term in (5.5)). Substituting from (5.4) into (5.5) the problem is to choose c_1 so as to maximise U. The first-order condition is

$$u'(c_1) - \rho p u'(c_2(0)) - \rho(1 - p)u'(c_2(y_2)) = 0 \qquad (5.6)$$

with the second-order condition requiring that

$$\Delta \equiv u''(c_1) + \rho^2 p u''(c_2(0)) + \rho^2(1 - p)u''(c_2(y_2)) < 0 \qquad (5.7)$$

which is certainly satisfied if the individual displays risk-aversion so that $u'' < 0$.

Before exploring the model and its solution based on (5.6) and (5.7) it is worth giving an economic interpretation to some of its features. Firstly the probability distribution of second-period income is based on just two values, 0 and y_2. It is useful to think of this as arising from a risk of job loss. In this case, the individual expects to lose the job with probability p and to remain employed with probability $(1 - p)$. The additive structure of total (intertemporal) utility given by (5.5) is harder to justify on any criterion other than on grounds of simplicity. However, the results stemming from this structure are not wildly at odds with intuition.

It is a straightforward matter (by total differentiation of (5.6)) to establish that *an increase in p lowers first-period consumption and hence increases savings*, while *an increase in either first-period income y_1 or second-period income if employed y_2 will reduce savings*. The effect of an increase in i or alternatively ρ is left as an exercise.

In the present context these results require nothing more than the concavity of the utility function. In more general models (referred to in the Bibliographic guide) relying neither on additive utility nor on our simple probability distribution of second-period income the results are not as clear cut. However, in some of these other models an increase in the riskiness of income has an effect similar to that of an increase in p here.

5.3   SAVINGS AND UNCERTAINTY IN RATE OF RETURN

Attention now focuses on uncertainty in the return to saving. In practice the variability of real interest rates (the interest rate net of the inflation rate) is a considerable source of uncertainty both because of volatile money markets and because of variation in price inflation. In interpreting the results of this section it does no harm to think of ρ as a real rate of return in this sense.

For simplicity we use the model of the last section but with $y_2 = 0$ in equation (5.3). In other words the emphasis is solely on how much of first-period income should be saved when the rate of return to saving is uncertain. Further we may be more general in the specification of the distribution of our random variable, now ρ, and use as our equivalent (5.5);

$$U(c_1, c_2) = u(c_1) + E[u(c_2)] \tag{5.8}$$

where the second term on the right-hand side of (5.8) is expected utility in the second period and the expectation is taken with respect to ρ. Finally, suppose that utility in each period may be written

$$u(c_i) = \frac{c_i^{\alpha}}{\alpha} \qquad 0 < \alpha < 1 \qquad i = 1, 2 \qquad (5.9)$$

It is easily established that $u' < 0$ and $u'' > 0$. Using (5.8) to choose c_1, the first-order condition is

$$u'(c_1) - E[\rho u'(\rho(y_1 - c_1))] = 0 \qquad (5.10)$$

and the second-order condition,

$$u''(c_1) + E[\rho^2 u''(\rho(y_1 - c_1))] < 0 \qquad (5.11)$$

The main finding of importance is that given our chosen form of $u(c)$ and the additive form of U *optimal consumption is higher and (therefore) optimal saving lower under rate of return uncertainty than under certainty.* The reader is encouraged to follow the ensuing sketch of a proof of this proposition.

Let c_1^* be the solution to (5.10). That is, c_1^* is the optimal consumption level under uncertainty. Now consider a certain world in which the certain rate of return happens to be equal to the expected rate of return in the uncertain case above. In the certain case the first-order condition is

$$u'(c_1) - E[\rho]u'(E[\rho](y_1 - c_1)) = 0$$

or

$$u'(c_1) - E[\rho]^{\alpha}(y_1 - c_1)^{\alpha - 1} = 0 \qquad (5.12)$$

and let $\hat{c}_1$ be the consumption level which satisfies (5.12).

Using (5.9), (5.10) and (5.12) we have,

$$u'(c_1^*) - (y_1 - c_1^*)^{\alpha - 1}E[\rho^{\alpha}] = 0 \qquad (5.13)$$

and

$$u'(\hat{c}) - (y_1 - \hat{c}_1)^{\alpha - 1}E[\rho]^{\alpha} = 0 \qquad (5.14)$$

Using a method of proof introduced in the last chapter, suppose we adopt the working hypothesis that $c_1^* = \hat{c}_1$ then inspection of (5.13) and (5.14) suggests that $E[\rho^{\alpha}] = \{E[\rho]\}^{\alpha}$. That this is *not* so is shown using a result known as *Jensen's inequality*;

if $\nu(x)$ is a concave function ($\nu'' < 0$) then $E[\nu(x)] < \nu\{E[x]\}$.

In our case $v(x) = x^\alpha$ with $0 < \alpha < 1$ and so $v(x)$ is indeed concave. Hence, by Jensen's inequality

$$E[\rho^\alpha] < \{E[\rho]\}^\alpha \tag{5.15}$$

Under the maintained hypothesis that $c_1^* = \hat{c}_1$, the inequality (5.15) implies that the left-hand side of (5.13) (lhs(5.13)) is greater than lhs(5.14). However, this contradicts the fact that lhs(5.13) = lhs(5.14) = 0. Assuming that (5.14) holds, the lhs(5.13) must be lowered towards equality with lhs(5.14), and we know from (5.11) that this is achieved by *raising* c_1^*. Thus our initial working hypothesis cannot be maintained and so $c_1^* > \hat{c}_1$ giving the result that consumption under uncertainty about rates of return on savings is greater than under certainty.

This result, although of some intuitive appeal, is hard to establish in more general cases. As will be pointed out in the Bibliographic guide our chosen form of $u(c)$ in (5.9) has a property which guarantees this result at least when U is additive.

5.4 PORTFOLIO CHOICE—AN INTRODUCTION

We have seen how the decision to abstain from consumption is affected by uncertainty of income and, of more relevance to the discussion of this section, by uncertainty in returns to saving. This section takes up this latter theme, but focuses attention not on how much to save but on how to save. In practice we face a large number of possible ways of holding our wealth over from one period to the next. We may buy government bonds, shares in quoted companies, real estate or simply choose to hold cash. Markets exist in each of these areas so that there is no difficulty in obtaining the asset we require—if the price is right! How do we choose?

From the point of view of uncertainty considerations the choice problem involves an assessment of likely (expected) returns associated with each alternative asset and the associated risk. The literature on the subject is large and occasionally complex but we are able to highlight some implications by using a relatively simple model.

Suppose we have a total wealth of W available to be held in the form of any asset we choose. For simplicity we choose our units so that $W = 1$ and assume that we may hold just two financial assets denoted m (money) and b (bonds) in any proportion we choose. Clearly $m = 1 - b$. If we choose to hold money in an interest-bearing account we will receive a certain rate of return of $(1 + i)$ on each unit held. The total return is therefore $(1 - b)(1 + i)$. The bond is sold after one period and it too produces a rate of return $(1 + i)$ per unit, but in addition there is a capital gain or loss resulting from the sale, the possibility of which must be taken into account when the bond is acquired. Assume with probability p the total worth of each bond will be $(1 + i + x)$ while with probability $(1 - p)$ it will be worth $(1 + i - x)$ where x is the capital gain or loss. The total expected value of the portfolio, money and bonds is,

$$p[(1 - b)(1 + i) + b(1 + i + x)] + (1 - p)[(1 - b)(1 + i) + b(1 + i - x)] = p[1 + i + bx] + (1 - p)[1 + i - bx]$$

while the expected utility is

$$U(b) = pu(1 + i + bx) + (1 - p)u(1 + i - bx) \qquad (5.16)$$

which is to be maximised by choosing b, the proportion of wealth held in bonds. The first-order condition is

$$pu'(1 + i + bx) - (1 - p)u'(1 + i - bx) = 0 \qquad (5.17)$$

with second-order condition

$$\Delta \equiv pxu''(1 + i + bx) + (1 - p)xu''(1 + i - bx) < 0 \qquad (5.18)$$

We may use (5.17) to answer the following question. Given p, what happens to the portfolio composition if the rate of interest i increases?

Total differentiation of (5.17) gives,

$$\frac{db}{di} = \{- pu''(1 + i + bx) + (1 - p)u''(1 + i - bx)\}/\Delta \qquad (5.19)$$

where $\Delta < 0$ is given by (5.18). Hence db/di is negative if the numerator in (5.19) is positive and db/di is positive if the numerator is negative. In particular,

$$\frac{db}{di} \gtrless 0 \quad \text{depending as} \quad \frac{u''(1 + i + bx)}{u''(1 + i - bx)} \gtrless \frac{(1 - p)}{p} \qquad (5.20)$$

Now $(1 - p)/p$ is a constant but $\lambda(b)$ defined as

$$\lambda(b) \equiv \frac{u''(1 + i + bx)}{u''(1 + i - bx)} \qquad (5.21)$$

depends on b. It is easily established that $\lambda'(b) < 0$ if $u''' > 0$, a condition consistent with (but not necessary for) decreasing absolute risk-aversion. Hence, $\lambda(b) > (1 - p)/p$ is associated with low values of b while $\lambda(b) < (1 - p)/p$ is associated with high values of b (assuming $u''' > 0$). The effect of an increase in i is therefore to increase the holdings of the risky asset if current holdings are modest and to lower the holdings of bonds if they occupy a large proportion of the portfolio.

The interest in this result is that although an increase in i increases the expected return on *both* assets it also affects their *relative* attractiveness. If relatively few bonds are held, an increase in the interest rate prompts an increase in bond holdings. Since b is 'small' the consequential increase in risk is small and, for the risk-averter, outweighed by the increased certain element of the portfolio return plus value of potential capital gains. On the other hand if bond holdings are already 'high' then the value of the certain return dominates and the individual moves out of the risky asset.

Beyond this, it is hard to obtain clear-cut results from general models of portfolio choice. For this reason, perhaps, the literature on this subject has been dominated by an exposition based on a special case. So famous and insightful is this approach that, despite some unsatisfactory features, I will discuss it briefly now.

5.5   PORTFOLIO CHOICE—FURTHER ANALYSIS

The special case is so constructed that the portfolio decision is based *solely* upon the *mean* and the *variance* of the distribution of portfolio returns. To continue in the spirit of the previous section, let there be just two assets. The riskless asset (money) has a certain return of $(1 + i)$ for each unit of money held whilst the risky asset (bonds) has an uncertain yield of $(1 + i + y)$ per bond where y is the capital gain or loss per bond and is uncertain. In the last section y took just two values, $+ x$ and $- x$, but in this section it may take a wide range of values. A portfolio as before is the way in which wealth $W(=1)$ is apportioned between the two assets.

It is convenient to define a new (random) variable, r, as being the total return when a proportion b of wealth is held in bonds. Continuing with the notation of the previous section we have,

$$r = (1 + i)m + (1 + i + y)b$$
$$= (1 + i)(1 - b) + (1 + i + y)b$$
$$r = (1 + i) + by \tag{5.22}$$

The mean portfolio return when b bonds are held is therefore

$$\mu \equiv E[r] = (1 + i) + bE[y] \tag{5.23}$$

and the variance of portfolio return is

$$\sigma^2 \equiv \text{VAR}[r] = E[r - \mu]^2$$
$$= E[(1 + i) + by - (1 + i) - bE[y]]^2$$
$$= b^2 E[y - E[y]]^2 \tag{5.24}$$

It is by no means obvious, however, that a von Neumann–Morgenstern agent whose behaviour was discussed in Chapter 3 would be able to make a portfolio decision on the basis of the mean and variance of portfolio returns alone, given in our case by (5.23) and (5.24), since such an agent would seek to maximise the expected utility of the portfolio return r, that is, to maximise

$$U(r) = E[u((1 + i) + by)] \tag{5.25}$$

and so the decision clearly depends on the distribution of y *and* the form of $u(.)$.

However, consider the (quadratic) utility function

$$u(r) = \alpha r + \beta r^2 \qquad \beta < 0 \tag{5.26}$$

This is increasing and concave in r for $r \leq (-\alpha/2\beta)$ and so (subject to a qualification discussed later) has the properties of a utility function displaying risk-aversion over a range of values of r. Combining (5.24) and (5.25) we have expected utility as,·

$$U(r) = E[\alpha r + \beta r^2] \qquad r \leq (-\alpha/2\beta) \tag{5.27}$$
$$= E[r] + \beta E[r^2]$$

Now $E[r]$ is simply μ given by (5.23). To shed some light on $E[r^2]$ we use a result from elementary statistics. The variance of r is given by

$$VAR[r] = E[r - \mu]^2$$
$$= E[r - E[r]]^2$$
$$= E\{[r - E[r]][r - E[r]]\}$$
$$= E\{r^2 - 2rE[r] + E[r]^2\}$$

and taking expectations gives

$$VAR[r] = E[r^2] - 2E[r]^2 + E[r]^2$$
$$= E[r^2] - E[r]^2$$

or

$$\sigma^2 = E[r^2] - E[r]^2$$

hence

$$E[r^2] = \sigma^2 + \mu^2 \qquad (5.28)$$

and so, using (5.27)

$$U(r) = \alpha\mu + \beta\mu^2 + \beta\sigma^2 \qquad (5.29)$$

Thus expected utility depends solely on the mean and variance of the distribution of portfolio returns.

We now have all the necessary ingredients for making a decision on the number of bonds to be held. A diagrammatic framework which will be familiar to undergraduate economists may be used. First notice that expected utility is increasing in the mean return μ over the relevant range and is decreasing in the variance of returns, as one would expect for a risk-averter. From (5.27)

$$\frac{dU(r)}{d\mu} = \alpha + 2\beta\mu > 0 \qquad \mu \lesseqgtr (-\alpha/2b) \qquad (5.30)$$

and

$$\frac{dU(r)}{d\sigma^2} = \beta < 0 \qquad (5.31)$$

because $\beta < 0$. Thus along a constant expected utility indifference curve,

$$\frac{d\sigma^2}{d\mu} = -\frac{[\alpha + 2\beta]}{\beta} > 0$$

and

$$\frac{d}{d\mu}\left(\frac{d\sigma^2}{d\mu}\right) = -2 < 0$$

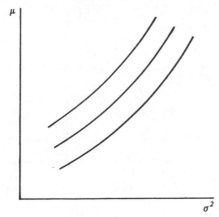

Figure 5.1: Mean–variance indifference curves

so that in a (μ, σ^2) diagram the indifference curves have the shapes illustrated in Figure 5.1.

In conventional consumer choice theory we are used to super-imposing on such an indifference map a 'budget constraint' which determines the 'feasible' combinations of goods given available income and prevailing prices. Although there is no 'budget constraint' as such in the present problem there is a set of 'feasible' combinations of mean return and variance of returns for various sizes of bond holdings. To derive this constraint we first investigate how μ and σ^2 change as b changes. Firstly, from (5.23)

$$\frac{d\mu}{db} = E[y] = \text{constant} > 0$$

and from (5.24)

$$\frac{d\sigma^2}{db} = 2bE[y - E[y]]^2 > 0$$

$$\frac{d}{db}\left(\frac{d\sigma^2}{db}\right) = 2E[y - E[y]]^2 > 0$$

These relationships are shown in Figure 5.2 frames (c) and (a).

The combination of μ and σ^2 as b increases is derived in frame (d) of Figure 5.2. At $\sigma^2 = 0$ no bonds are held and the total (certain) return is $(1 + i)$. An increase in σ^2 and in μ away from this point are associated with a larger and larger number of bonds being held.

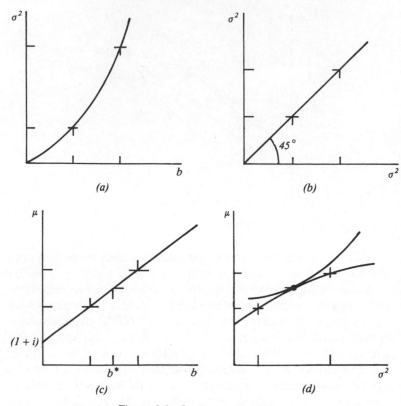

Figure 5.2: Optimum portfolio

However, as the curve is concave, unit increases in bond holdings add more to risk (measured by variance) than they do to mean return.

Frame (d) of Figure 5.2 superimposes the indifference map onto the constraint curve and the optimal portfolio mean–variance combination, implying a particular proportion of bonds held, b^* is given by the tangency of an indifference curve with the constraint curve. Hence it appears that a risk-averter will hold some wealth in the form of a risky asset.

Of some interest is the question of what happens to the relative proportions of money and bonds held if the (certain) interest rate i increases. Figure 5.3 reproduces frame (d) of Figure 5.2 and shows that an increase in i shifts the constraint curve upwards, giving a

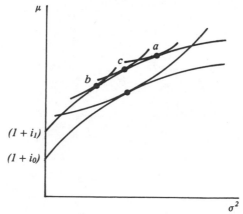

Figure 5.3: Effect of an increase in $i(i_1 > i_0)$

higher mean return for each level of risk. (It is clear from (5.23) and (5.27) that i affects μ but not σ^2.) However, the new equilibrium may be at a higher level of risk (point a) implying an increase in bond holdings, a lower level of risk (point b) implying a lower level of bond holdings, or an unchanged level of risk (point c), implying no change in bond holdings. Thus even a risk-averter (whose measure of risk is the variance of returns) may increase bond holdings when the certain rate of return (on money) rises.

The reason for this ambiguity, as in conventional consumer indifference analysis, is the existence of two effects which combine to make up the changes between equilibrium. A 'wealth effect' (corresponding to the familiar 'income effect') determines the effect on the number of bonds held of having the expected portfolio return on all potential portfolios increased. This effect alone may lead to more or fewer bonds being held depending on exactly how μ and σ^2 are weighted in the utility function or on the degree of risk-aversion. In Figure 5.3 this is reflected on the precise configuration of the indifference map. On the other hand a 'substitution effect' operates to increase the holdings of the *relatively* higher-yielding asset. In the case of Figure 5.3 the substitution effect is zero because all portfolio combinations are affected equally and at the margin there is no change in the relative attractiveness of one portfolio over another. However, suppose that the expected capital gains per bond $E[y]$ increased with the certain interest rate unchanged. This is illustrated in Figure 5.4 where the overall 'no change' move from

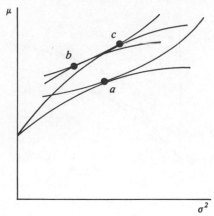

Figure 5.4: Effect of an increase in $E[y]$

a to c has two effects. The wealth effect is from a to b and is negative so that 'risk' is an 'inferior good' in the special sense of consumer theory. However at each level of risk (bond-holding) the 'terms of trade' between risk and expected payoff have increased so that the taking on of slightly more risk increases the expected payoff by more than previously. Thus at the margin the increase in $E[y]$ increases the relative attractiveness of more risky portfolios, and so on the basis of the 'substitution effect' alone a higher expected return per bond increases the desired number of bonds held. As drawn, the wealth effect (a to b) resulting from an increase in all portfolio yields (except the 'no risk' portfolio) is just offset by the substitution effect (b to c) resulting from the increased *relative* attractiveness of higher-risk portfolio.

Using the framework we might investigate the effect of an increase in the variance of bond returns. This is left as an exercise.

The mean–variance approach outlined here has been used widely in portfolio analysis, but there are difficulties in reconciling the behaviour of von Neumann–Morgenstern agents and those whose decisions rest solely on the mean and variance of returns. The problem is not resolved satisfactorily by assuming a quadratic utility function defined over a restricted range of r. Consider (5.26) once more;

$$u(r) = \alpha r + \beta r^2 \qquad \beta < 0 \qquad (5.26)$$

and calculate the index of absolute risk-aversion (defined in chapter three) as

$$R_A(r) = -\frac{2\beta}{\alpha + 2\beta r} \qquad (5.32)$$

However,

$$R_A{}'(r) = \frac{4\beta^2}{[\alpha + 2\beta r]^2} \qquad (5.33)$$

says that the quadratic utility function displays *increasing* absolute risk-aversion. As we saw in section 3.6, however, *decreasing* absolute risk-aversion would appear to reflect behaviour more accurately. In this respect the quadratic form of utility function is deficient. Abandoning the quadratic form of the utility and remaining within the mean–variance approach is possible only if attention is restricted to distribution of returns which may be characterised solely in terms of the mean and the variance. The 'normal distribution' is an example of this. When there is more than one risky asset the normal distribution is the only two-parameter distribution of individual asset yield that combines to give a two-parameter distribution of total portfolio yield.

The applicability of the mean–variance approach *within* the expected utility framework is apparently limited and contentious. Despite this, however, the approach is widely used and produces results which on the whole are not greatly at odds with intuition.

5.6   CONCLUSION

Although quite 'special' the models of this chapter have illustrated how uncertainty may play an important role in allocating an individual's resources between consumption and savings, and between various forms of savings. In the latter case an important finding is that even a risk-averter will generally hold a portion of a portfolio in a risky asset.

5.7   BIBLIOGRAPHIC GUIDE

The models of sections 5.2 and 5.3 are simplifications of more general models discussed in Hey (1979). A fuller account of the model of section 5.3 is to be found in Lippman and McCall (1981) where it is apparent that the result that consumption under interest rate uncertainty is greater than under certainty is readily available because the utility function in (5.9) is of the constant relative risk-aversion type. The reader might verify that this is so. The standard reference on the portfolio choice models is Tobin (1958) though a recent exposition by Ford (1983) gives a full account. The main area in which portfolio theory has found application is in monetary theory and details may be found in any text on monetary theory including Goodhart (1975).

5.8   EXERCISES

5.1   Use the model of section 5.2 to investigate the effect of an increase in the interest rate on savings.

5.2   Use the model of section 5.5 to investigate the effect of an increase in the variance of bond returns on portfolio composition.

5.3   Show that if the distribution of bond returns is normal, then expected utility depends only on μ and σ^2.

5.4   Using Figure 5.3 explain what is happening as we move from the initial equilibrium to point a, and to point b. The move to point c is discussed in the text.

5.5   Using the analysis of section 5.6 discuss what may happen if VAR[y] increases.

6. State-contingent and Futures Markets

6.1 INTRODUCTION

As we have seen, ultimate consequences of actions taken under uncertainty result only when the state of the world has been resolved, and so far we have looked at a number of problems facing individuals in fairly typical market settings. In this chapter, and in the next, we take a look at markets which have a key role in making complete the possibilities open to individuals in risky environments.

Insurance markets are a classic example. In addition to taking everyday decisions in the sale and purchase of commodities, people generally take out insurance policies as protection in case of adverse events. For example, the purchase of a cooker in the cooker market may well be accompanied by the taking out of a service agreement which specifies for a given initial payment 'free' service and repairs for the appliance for a particular period—in effect, *insurance* against the occurrence of faults. Although the 'purchase' of such an agreement or contract may be regarded by many people as part of the cooker purchase it is conceptually distinct and involves quite different considerations. The cooker purchase has something to do with the (constrained) satisfaction of cullinery wants or needs while the insurance cover is the result of a desire to avoid taking risk with adversity.

Hence there appears to be a role for markets in which individuals may spread their risk by paying out in favourable times and receiving incomes in otherwise unfavourable times. In the same way that we choose between one consumer good and another we may choose between one income or consumption bundle in one state of the world and another income or consumption bundle in an alternative state of the world. If there are willing suppliers of contracts of this type and if a price can be agreed then there is a market. Markets of this type are often known as markets in *state-contingent claims*. In the following section we set up a framework for the analysis of state-contingent markets. In section 6.3 we look at the role of the stock market as a way of spreading risks, and in section 6.4 we provide an introductory analysis of futures markets. The analysis of insurance markets is conducted separately in Chapter 7.

6.2   STATE-CONTINGENT MARKETS

State-contingent markets may be markets in incomes, assets or goods. The market analysis may be conducted using quite standard techniques as long as we bear in mind not only that goods with different characteristics are distinct, but that items under different states of the world and at different times are also distinct.

We start by considering income to be received in two states of the world, y_1 and y_2. If income is the same in both states of the world then we have complete certainty in the sense that if $y_1 = y_2$ it does not matter which state of the world eventuates (as long as we are only interested in income). Hence, a *certainty line* drawn in a (y_1, y_2) diagram showing all points at which $y_1 = y_2$ is a 45° ray from the origin. This is illustrated in Figure 6.1.

Now consider point x^1. At this point income in state 1 exceeds income in state 2, $y_1 > y_2$ so that the individual is worse off in state 2. At point x^2, however, $y_1 < y_2$ and it is state 1 which is less

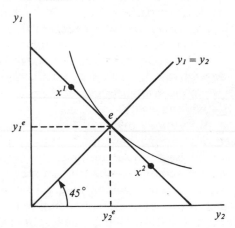

Figure 6.1: A market in state-contingent claims

desirable. A market in state-contingent claims enables us to exchange income in favourable states of the world for increased income in poor states, and we may exchange in this way until we reach the certainty line. To illustrate suppose our initial endowment of state-contingent income is x^1 in Figure 6.1. We may dislike the idea that we are potentially so much worse off in state 2 that we would buy a contract from a third party who promises to provide (for the contract price) a supplement to income should state 2 occur. In the event of state 1 occurring we receive nothing but of course we have paid out the contract price. Effectively we have traded income in state 1 for additional income in state 2. The rate of exchange between y_1 and y_2 of course depends on the contract price. If each unit of y_1 spent on a contract results in an increase in y_2 of α then the price of each unit of y_2 is $1/\alpha$ and the opportunities for trading y_1 for y_2 are represented by a straight line with slope $-1/\alpha$. In Figure 6.1 I have assumed that the opportunities for trading y_1 for y_2 are represented by the line (x^1, x^2) extending to the axes. This line shows the *possibilities* for trading state-contingent incomes. However, exactly where along the opportunity line we would settle depends on our preferences between state-contingent incomes. If our preferences are represented by convex indifference curves then an equilibrium is represented by an equality of the marginal terms of trade and the marginal rate of substitution between state-contingent incomes. Although not necessarily the case such an equilibrium may occur on the certainty line, and this case is illustrated in Figure 6.1 with equilibrium at e.

It is important to remember that whilst the equilibrium at e in Figure 6.1 is reminiscent of the traditional consumer choice problem, there is one important difference. In consumer choice with y_1 and y_2 representing two distinct commodities, the equilibrium determines how much of each good is to be consumed. The consumption of one commodity does not exclude the consumption of the other good totally. In the analysis of state-contingent claims, however, only *one* state of the world will be realised and the receipt of income in one state of the world excludes the receipt of income in the other. Thus we receive *either* y_1^e *or* y_2^e depending on which state of the world obtains. In Figure 6.1 we are simply stating that, given the initial endowment and the opportunities for trading incomes, we prefer the *alternatives* offered at e to those offered at x^1 or x^2.

The framework developed in Figure 6.1 will be of some assistance in the analysis of this chapter and of Chapter 7. However, we will be focusing more on the opportunities for and constraints on trading in state-contingent claims rather than on the preference structure. The reason for this emphasis is that often the scope for state-contingent trading is limited. We intend to discover why.

6.3   STOCK MARKETS

We are interested in the stock market as a vehicle by which income risk may be reduced by exchanging state-contingent claims. Stock markets may be viewed from two angles as performing two roles. Firstly, from the production side, stock markets are a way by which firms raise investment capital in such a way that the entrepreneur personally does not shoulder the entire financial liability of the corporation. Secondly, purchasers of stocks and shares in companies see the activity as one of portfolio diversification, though one with an element of risk since the income from the portfolio is intimately linked with the fortunes of the companies whose shares are represented in the portfolio. Whilst the first of these functions of the stock market is interesting and may be used to answer questions on the appropriate debt–equity structure for companies, it is the second function which occupies us here.

Suppose that there are two firms and two states of the world. Denote by π_i^j company j's profit in state of the world i; $j = 1, 2$; $i = 1, 2$. Each firm floats a total of N^j shares on the market at price v^j and the total stock market value of each firm is therefore $V^j = v^j N^j$; $j = 1, 2$. We are interested in the behaviour of an individual who inherits a number of shares in each company and who may adjust the portfolio. As we noted before we are interested in the opportunities for portfolio (and hence 'income') adjustment rather than the individual's preference structure. A holding of a proportion β^j of company j's N^j shares entitles an individual to the same share of profits. Hence, an individuals income in state of the work i is;

$$y_i = \beta^1 \pi_i^1 + \beta^2 \pi_i^2 \qquad i = 1, 2 \qquad (6.1)$$

Finally denote by $\hat{\beta}^j$ the initially endowed proportion of firm j's shares held, then exchanges in the shares must be such that the preferred share purchases cost no more than the total receipts from the sale of the initial endowment. In fact, I assume that the following budget constraint must hold

$$v^1\beta^1N^1 + v^2\beta^2N^2 = v^1\hat{\beta}^1N^1 + v^2\hat{\beta}^2N^2 \qquad (6.2)$$

or,

$$v^1N^1(\beta^1 - \hat{\beta}^1) = -v^2N^2(\beta^2 - \hat{\beta}^2) \qquad (6.3)$$

or,

$$V^1(\beta^1 - \hat{\beta}^1) = -V^2(\beta^2 - \hat{\beta}^2) \qquad (6.4)$$

In the following analysis I constrain the β^js to be non-negative. This may not appear to be much of a constraint, but there is a sense in which a negative number of shares may be 'bought', so that $\beta^j < 0$, for firm j's shares. This phenomenon, which actually occurs in stock markets, is known as 'selling short'. That is, a seller of shares sells more shares than he or she has. For a time the individual therefore owes shares and only supplies the deficit shares when asked to do so. In the interim the receipts from short sales are invested elsewhere, hopefully in a highly rewarding portfolio, and then shares in the company concerned are bought and resold to satisfy the deficit created by short selling. For the moment, however, we assume that this type of behaviour is not allowed.

Opportunities for trading state-contingent incomes in this stock market are derived in Figure 6.2. Suppose that the individual sells all the initial endowment of firm 2 shares and buys all firm 1 shares. The maximum possible proportion of firm 1 shares which may be acquired is denoted β_0^1. Now in each state of the world i the individual's income if only firm 1 shares are held is given by the product of the properties of shares held and the profit in each state of the world π_i.

The profit vector of firm 1 $\pi^1 = (\pi_1^1, \pi_2^1)$ is shown in Figure 6.2 by the ray $(0, \pi^1)$, and the maximum income in state 1 if only firm 1 shares are held is $\beta_0^1\pi_1^1$ while that in state 2 is $\beta_0^1\pi_2^1$. Similarly the coordinates $(\beta_0^2\pi_1^2, \beta_0^2\pi_2^2)$ give the maximum income vector if only firm 2 shares are held. By diversifying the portfolio so that shares in both firms are held any state-contingent income pair along the line (a, b) is possible. Of course, one of these is the initial-endowment–income pair at point $\hat{y}$, which is constructed using the

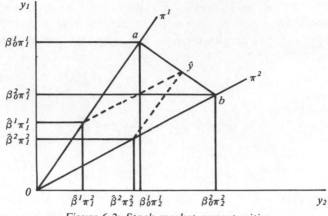

Figure 6.2: Stock market opportunities

parallelogram rule of vector addition. Thus trading shares makes
movements away from y toward a or toward b possible in accord-
ance with the preferences of the individual. Figure 6.3 illustrates a
preferred income pair at y when the initial endowment is $\hat{y}$.

An important feature of this analysis is that income pairs to the
'north-west' of π^1 and to the 'south-east' of π^2 are not available
to this individual, and the opportunity line (a, b) does not extend
into these regions. This is an important result because it means that
the stock market provides *incomplete* opportunities for state-

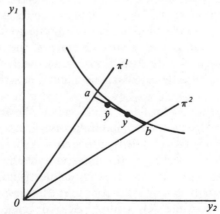

Figure 6.3: Individual's preferred allocation of claims

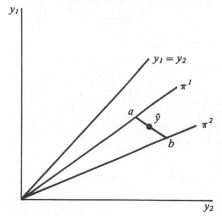

Figure 6.4: Non-availability of riskless stock portfolio

contingent income claims. To see the importance of this, suppose we wanted to hold a riskless portfolio in the sense that the state-contingent incomes were equal. The desired position would be analagous to that depicted in Figure 6.1. However, suppose the profit vectors were those shown in Figure 6.4, with the state-contingent income opportunity line a, b. In this case no riskless portfolio is possible.

In general the range of state-contingent income possibilities depends on the diversity of the firms' profit vectors—the further apart are π^1 and π^2 the greater are the increased income opportunities. Of course, if the π^1 and π^2 vectors coincide with the y_1 and y_2 axes respectively, the full range of state-contingent income claims is available and the stock market replicates all the opportunities presented by a pure state-contingent market. At the other extreme if the π^1 and π^2 vectors coincide with each other (so that $\pi_i^1 = \alpha\pi_i^2$, $i = 1$, 2) then there are *no* opportunities for exchanging state-contingent incomes. Stock markets with linearly dependent profit vectors reduce risk-spreading opportunities.

One way of extending the opportunities where the situation is like that in Figure 6.2 is somehow to extend the opportunities line (a, b) towards the axes in each direction. This is achievable by 'selling short'. For example, by selling short on company 1's shares more than the previous maximum number of company 2's shares may be bought and the individual is able to move beyond point b

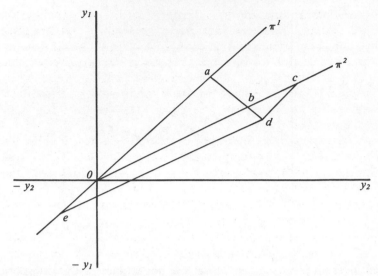

Figure 6.5: Opportunities with limited 'selling short'

on the $(0, \pi^2)$ vector in Figure 6.2. The position is illustrated in Figure 6.5 where c is the new attainable point if some selling short on company 1's shares generates income to buy company 2's shares.

Applying the parallellogram rule shows that (a, b) is extended to (a, d) as a result of short selling shares of firm 1. The extent of short sales is given by $(0, e)$. Further selling short may extend a, b towards the y_2 axis. Similarly selling short the shares of company 2 may extend the opportunity line a, b towards the y axis. Short selling effectively extends opportunities by relaxing the budget constraint, and in this way produces a complete range of state-contingent claims possibilities.

6.4 FUTURES MARKETS

Futures markets also extend the range of trading possibilities and are common both in markets for financial assets and in primary commodity markets.

We take as the focus for our discussion the opportunities facing a cereal farmer. The output to be produced by the farmer for sale 'next period' is uncertain, as is the price that the output will bring in the market. Of course, the output uncertainty and the price uncertainty are connected, since in general for a given demand structure large outputs will sell for low prices and small outputs for high prices. Denote by p_1^s the uncertain next period price or *future spot price*. The current market price of cereal is not uncertain and is referred to as the *current spot price*. The *expected* future spot price is denoted $\bar{p}_1^s$.

A *futures market*, for cereal in this case, is described in the following way. Given output and future price uncertainty, the farmer may choose to contract to supply an amount of cereal, say x, to the market next period at a known price, say p_0^f. The price p_0^f is determined in the market for futures contracts of this type and is not controlled by any individual farmer. Naturally p_0^f equates the (expected) demand for cereal next period with the total of all xs promised by the producers to be delivered to the market next period. The notation p_0^f serves to emphasise that the agreed price is determined in the current period, period 0, but applies to quantities currently contracted for delivery in the following period. This price is often known as the *forward price*, or *futures price*.

Two questions naturally arise in markets of this type. Firstly, given that actual output next period is currently unknown, how does the chosen value of x compare with the expected output next period? Secondly, how does the currently determined futures market price p_0^f compare with $\bar{p}_1^s$, the expected spot price for the next period?

To investigate the first question we set up the decision problem for the typical cereal farmer. Recall that both the future spot price and output for cereal are uncertain. In the language of Chapter 2 we could say that they depend on the state of the world. To show this dependence when there are many (say n) states of the world we write the future spot price when the state of the world is θ, say $p_1^s(\theta)$, $\theta = 1, \ldots, n$. Similarly next period's output when the state of the world is θ as $q_1(\theta)$, $\theta = 1, \ldots, n$. Utility next period in any state of the world depends on the total income generated by the sale of output, which for a sufficiently 'small' (i.e. price-taking) producer is the sum of revenue from output sold on the next periods' spot market and that delivered on the futures market. Since an amount x is committed to the futures market, this leaves only $q_1(\theta) - x$ for delivery to the spot market. Hence total income when the state of the world is θ, is:

$$y(\theta) = p_1^s(\theta)[q_1(\theta) - x] + p_0^f x$$
$$= p_1^s(\theta)q_1(\theta) + x[p_0^f - p_1^s(\theta)] \tag{6.5}$$

and expected utility is,

$$U = \underset{\theta}{E}\{u[y(\theta)]\}$$
$$= \underset{\theta}{E}\{u(p_1^s(\theta)q(\theta) + x[p_0^f - p_1^s(\theta)])\} \tag{6.6}$$

The optimal choice of x requires,

$$\underset{\theta}{E}\{u'[y(\theta)][p_0^f - p_1^s(\theta)]\} = 0 \tag{6.7}$$

A detailed analysis of (6.7) is outside the scope of this book but some intuitively plausible results are available. The reader is asked to take these on trust for now and follow up the derivations in the references to be given later. First we need some additional terminology. If the farmer decides to sell the entire expected output on the futures market so that $x = \bar{q}_1 (\equiv \underset{\theta}{E}q_1(\theta))$ then the farmer is said to be perfectly hedged. If $0 < x < \bar{q}_1$ the farmer is partially hedged. If $x > \bar{q}_1$ the farmer is over-committed. Finally if $x < 0$, so that the intention is to *buy* on the futures market, then the farmer is said to be in a speculative position. Notice that the case where $x > \bar{q}_1$ is akin to the 'selling short' position in the stock market model of the previous section. Also notice that all of these positions are *ex ante* positions, and because q_1 is uncertain they might not reflect the actual position that eventuates. For example, a farmer who, at the time of taking the decision opts for the perfectly hedged position, $x = \bar{q}_1$, may find that there is an over-commitment *ex post* so that $x > q_1$. In this case and in any case of *ex post* over-commitment the farmer must honour the futures contract and buy on the spot market in order to make up the shortfall. Similarly in the case where $x < q_1$ residual of output not pre-committed to the futures contract is sold on the spot market.

As a special case, suppose that price is random but that output is not. All income variability is therefore due to prices. In this case, regardless of the farmers' attitude to risk,

a perfectly hedged, overcommitted, or partially hedged

position is adopted when $p_0^f = \bar{p}_1^s$, $p_0^f > \bar{p}_1^s$ or $p_0^f < \bar{p}_1^s$ respectively.

As another example suppose $p_0^f = \bar{p}_1^s$ then

$x \gtreqless 0$ depending as $\text{cov}(p_1^s q_1, p_1^s) \gtreqless 0$.

Roughly speaking this amounts to the statement that a farmer will hedge or speculate on the futures market depending on whether revenue and prices on the spot market are postively or negatively correlated.

These results make use of various assumptions about the relationship between the forward price and the expected spot price. Thus, we turn to the second question, what is the likely relationship between p_0^f and $\bar{p}_1^s$ in market equilibrium? Much here depends on who the market participants are, but the following result appears to be intuitively plausible.

The futures prices is less that the expected spot price $(p_0^f < \bar{p}_1^s)$ if farmers are risk-averse.

This idea is clearly related to that of the risk premium discussed in Chapter 3. Farmers who are risk-averse are prepared to trade at a certain price somewhat lower than the expected value of a random price. This is clearly a measure of how keen cereal farmers are to avoid price (and hence income) uncertainty.

Whether the futures price is in fact a downward-biased estimator of the spot price in many futures markets is, of course, an empirical issue. However, *if* true it raises some interesting questions relating to the workings of 'efficient markets'. Intuitively we may feel that agents somewhat less risk-averse than farmers may enter the market where $p_0^f < \bar{p}_1^s$ and exploit the arbitrage possibilities of buying on the futures to sell on the spot. In this case, with perfect arbitrage, the equality of the futures price and the spot price seems inevitable. This is a complex and fascinating issue which may be readily followed up in the Bibliographic guide.

6.5 CONCLUSION

This chapter has provided an introduction to markets which arise purely or largely to avoid undesirable risks. The following chapter takes up the state-contingent claims model, introduced in section 6.2 to study the risk-reducing role of insurance markets.

6.6 BIBLIOGRAPHIC GUIDE

The model of section 6.3 is based on an exposition of exchange possibilities in stock markets by Gravelle and Rees (1981) where a more complete mathematical specification of the model may be found. An analysis of the stock market with production is to be found in Diamond (1967).

The model of the cereal farmer of section 6.4 used results from Stiglitz (1983). Other papers in the volume edited by Streit (1983) would be useful starting points for those interested in futures markets. A comprehensive treatment of the effects of risk on primary commodity markets is to be found in Newbury and Stiglitz (1981).

6.7 EXERCISES

6.1 Using the model of state-contingent claims underlying figure 6.1, establish that for a given set of exchange possibilities an individual need not necessarily prefer to be in a 'certain-income' equilibrium. Is this behaviour inconsistent with risk-aversion?

6.2 In the model of stock market exchange possibilities of section 6.3, demonstrate that when firms' profits are linearly dependent there are no opportunities for the exchange of state-contingent incomes. Interpret.

6.3 Explain why 'selling short' expands the set of exchange possibilities in the stock market.

6.4 What factors, in general, will determine whether a producer of a primary product will hedge on the futures market?

6.5 Why do futures markets not exist for *all* commodities? Why is there not a complete set of futures markets?

7. Insurance Markets

7.1 INTRODUCTION

Most of us, at some time, make insurance decisions and it is obvious that insurance is a response to uncertainty or to risky situations. It is less obvious that the techniques developed in earlier chapters lend themselves ideally to the analysis of insurance decisions and the nature of equilibrium in insurance markets.

To start the analysis I develop in the following section a simple model of the decision which leads an individual to purchase insurance. This section *assumes* for this purpose that a market for insurance exists in that there are willing suppliers and a market price at which insurance contracts are traded. The analysis of the individual demander of insurance is relatively straightforward. However, some difficulties arise when we stand back and look at a large group of potential demanders from the point of view of a potential seller in possession of little information about individuals. By and large it is these difficulties, which are usually referred to as '*moral hazard*' and '*adverse selection*', which make insurance markets worthy of particular attention. For this reason the analysis of market equilibrium in section 7.4 is preceded by a study of these problems.

7.2 INDIVIDUAL INSURANCE DECISIONS

The basis for our model of the individual demander of insurance is the single-period model of expected utility maximisation much used in previous chapters. In general people find it worthwhile to buy insurance protection when there is a small probability of large losses being incurred.

In this section we assume that there is a ready supply of insurance contracts and focus attention on the demand for insurance. There are two models to be considered. In the first we examine the decision of whether to insure against a particular financial loss completely or not to insure at all. This is in the nature of an 'all-or-nothing' decision for the individual. The issue here is the level of insurance premium which would just be sufficient to induce the taking out of an insurance policy. In the second model, the individual determines not the price at which insurance contracts may be bought but the extent of the cover to be taken. Although the second model conforms closely to the actual circumstances faced by most people, the first model is a useful starting point.

(a) The demand for full cover

Consider an individual with an initial wealth of W facing the risk of a financial loss $x(< W)$ with probability p. If no insurance is taken out the individual's expected utility is given by,

$$U_0 = pu(W - x) + (1 - p)u(W) \qquad (7.1)$$

However, suppose that by paying a premium h the individual may insure fully against the loss. Rather than suffer a loss x with probability p, the individual would rather pay an amount h for certain, knowing that with probability p there will be a loss of x but also the immediate receipt of x from the insurance policy. Expected utility with the all-cover policy is

$$U_I = pu(W - h) + (1 - p)u(W - h)$$
$$= u(W - h) \qquad (7.2)$$

Now, for an expected utility maximiser choosing to take out insurance the expected utility, U_I (7.2) should be certainly no less than U_0 in (7.1). It is clear that the utility from taking out insurance falls as the premium rises, so that

$$\frac{dU_I}{dh} = - u'(W - h) < 0 \qquad (7.3)$$

where $u'(.)$, the marginal utility of wealth is positive. Hence, the *maximum* that an individual will pay for insurance, h^*, satisfies

$$u(W - h^*) = pu(W - x) + (1 - p)u(W) \qquad (7.4)$$

Equation (7.4) tells us that the utility from full insurance, or alternatively the utility from removing income uncertainty, is a weighted average of the utility from full wealth and the utility from the net wealth after a financial loss. It follows that

$$u(W - x) < u(W - h^*) < u(W) \qquad (7.5)$$

and so,

$$h^* < x \qquad (7.5)'$$

In what follows we will specify behaviour as being that of a risk-averter, so that $u''(.) < 0$. Differentiation of (7.4) gives the following results,

$$\frac{dh^*}{dp} = \frac{u(W - x) - u(W)}{-u'(W - h^*)} > 0 \qquad (7.6)$$

(The denominator in (7.6) is negative by (7.3) and the numerator is negative by (7.5).)

$$\frac{dh^*}{dx} = \frac{pu'(W - x)}{u'(W - h^*)} > 0 \qquad (7.7)$$

The maximum premium that an expected utility maximiser would pay for full insurance cover increases with the probability of loss and with the size of the loss. The effect of an increase in initial wealth is left as an exercise. Notice that since we have defined h^* as the maximum premium to be paid for full cover, it is the maximum that the individual would see deducted from certain wealth in order to avoid the 'gamble' of losing x with probability p—the definition we gave for the *risk premium* in Chapter 3.

That the full-cover premium is less than the loss, as stated in (7.5)', is obvious enough; however, using the properties of a risk-averse utility function we are able to go further. Recall from Chapter 3 that for a risk-averse individual the utility of the expected value of a lottery exceeds the expected utility of the lottery, or in the context of this section

$$u(p(W - x) + (1 - p)W) > pu(W - x) + (1 - p)u(W) \qquad (7.8)$$

for a risk averter. Using (7.8) in (7.4) gives

$$u(W - h^*) < u(p(W - x) + (1 - p)W) \qquad (7.9)$$

or

$$u(W - h^*) < u(W - px) \qquad (7.10)$$

and so,

$$h^* > px \qquad (7.11)$$

The risk-averse expected utility maximiser is prepared to pay an insurance premium in excess of the expected value of the loss.

(b)   The insurance deductible

In the model of the previous section the individual was presented with a choice between no insurance and full insurance against a financial loss and chose the maximum 'price' of the insurance contract. In practice, and in the model of this section, the circumstances facing individuals are somewhat different. To keep matters at their simplest I assume that *some* insurance (though not necessarily full insurance) is preferred to no insurance. The *premium h* is determined by the insuring firm according to a known formula to be outlined presently. The individual's choice is to determine the *extent* of the insurance cover. That is, the insured individual determines how much of the loss x may be reclaimed from the insurer, say an amount y. The difference between the loss x and the claim y is known as the *deductible*, D, so that

$$D \equiv x - y \tag{7.12}$$

In the model of this section the risk-averse individual chooses $D > 0$ and therefore does not opt for full cover. To demonstrate this interesting result we extend the model of the previous section. The premium h is now determined by the insurer according to a formula known to the insured. In particular the insurer makes a policy available at its expected cost, and in addition to the expected payout of a policy with cover y, py, there is an administrative cost of k per payout. The total expected cost to the insurer of providing a cover y is therefore

$$e = py + pky \tag{7.13}$$

Assuming that $h = e$ and making use of (7.12) gives,

$$h = p(1 + k)(x - D) \tag{7.14}$$

Expected utility is now given by

$$U_D = pu(W - x + y - h) + (1 - p)u(W - h) \tag{7.15}$$

or, again using (7.12)

$$U_D = pu(W - D - h) + (1 - p)u(W - h) \tag{7.16}$$

Choosing D in (7.16) bearing in mind the dependence of h on D in (7.14) gives, from the first-order condition,

$$\frac{u'(W - D^* - h)}{u'(W - h)} = \frac{(1 - p)(1 + k)}{1 - p(1 + k)} \qquad (7.17)$$

The right-hand side of (7.17) is greater than unity and hence

$$u'(W - D^* - h) > u'(W - h) \qquad (7.18)$$

which, by concavity of $u(.)$ for the risk-averter implies

$$W - D^* - h < W - h$$

or

$$D^* > 0$$

It is optimal for the risk-averter to choose a positive deductible and so the individual does not fully insure, but insures fully above a deductible. Thus the individual pays the premium $h = p(1 + k)(x - D^*)$ and has the deductible written into the insurance contract. The insured person only makes a claim on the policy if the loss exceeds D^* and then the claim is only the difference between the loss and the deductible.

This result depends critically on the relationship between the price of insurance (the premium) and the coverage, given by (7.14). (By claiming only above a deductible the individual is able to keep insurance costs down.) Clearly this involves a trade-off, between the increase in cover and the cost of cover, and not surprisingly the balance is struck where the expected utility gain from extra cover equals the expected utility cost in terms of the premium.

A slight modification to this model of the deductible will lead us naturally into the discussion of the next section. Suppose that the insurance terms are agreed as before but that the insurance company, in calculating the premium (based remember on expected cost), is not able to identify p the probability of loss for a particular individual, but rather uses an average probability for the appropriate group of individuals, say $\bar{p}$. In practice $\bar{p}$ will be calculated from the insurer's actuarial tables. The individual maximises expected utility as before by choosing the deductible D; however, this time (7.14) is written,

$$h = \bar{p}(1 + k)(x - D) \qquad (7.19)$$

and so (7.17) is modifed slightly to

$$\frac{u'(W - D^* - h)}{u'(W - h)} = \frac{(1 - p)(1 + k)}{1 - \bar{p}(1 + k)} \tag{7.20}$$

Now consider two individuals in the group who differ only in their personal loss probabilities, p_1 and p_2, with $p_1 > p_2$. (You can think of the average of these probabilities being equal to $\bar{p}$ so that $\bar{p} = (p_1 + p_2)/2$.) The individuals are otherwise identical and the insurers are unable to distinguish the 'p_1-person' from the 'p_2-person'. A simple comparative-static exercise which is left to the reader establishes that.

$$\frac{dD^*}{dp} < 0 \quad \text{for given } \bar{p} \tag{7.21}$$

Hence the individual with the higher probability of loss chooses a lower deductible. A person who regards a loss as being quite likely will then opt for greater insurance cover. Now, insuring firms do observe the deductible chosen by people to have written into their insurance contract, so that a systematic relationship between a person's own risk evaluation and choice of deductible gives the insurer an indication of an individual's loss probability. An individual's risk of loss p is not observable to the insurer but the revealed choice of deductible, D, is and provides the insuring firm with information on whether the applicant is an acceptable risk. This identification of types of individuals solely on the basis of their response to market conditions is known as *self-selection*. The models of this section have assumed that individuals have no control of either the size of the financial loss, x, or the probability of it occurring. If these assumptions do not hold and if the insurance premium is only tentatively related to the individual's choice of contractual arrangement quite different behaviour from that underlying self-selection may result. This behaviour, which is problematic both for the insuring firm and for the market equilibrium, is discussed now.

7.3 MORAL HAZARD AND RELATED PROBLEMS

Moral hazard arises when individuals have some control over either the probability of or magnitude of the loss but changes in these controls are not observed by the insurer and do not affect the premium. In these circumstances there are incentives for 'over-insurance'. This need not take the form of excessive coverage on a single policy but may involve multiple policies with different companies. This, of course, is expensive in terms of the premiums to be paid out but may be a worthwhile investment if the probability of loss is deliberately augmented. Alternatively 'moral hazard' may take the form of a relaxing of security measures because of the insurance cover. Either way moral hazard concerns the effect on the expected loss, which is partly under the control of the individual in the presence of insurance.

Whether moral hazard is present or not, a market composed of many individuals who vary in their risk liability but who cannot be individually identified by an insurer in any systematic way must face the same contract opportunities and the same premium and must opt for the same cover. Hence good-risk and bad-risk types all pay the same premium but the latter group by definition receive more from claims on insurance policies than does the former group. If these claims are large the average premium may have to rise so that the insuring firm can maintain its profits and the net losses to the good risks increase further. Some good risks may leave the market and others may succumb to the moral hazard temptations. The result is a market containing only bad-risk individuals. This problem is often referred to as *adverse selection* and this interesting phenomenon makes a front-of-stage appearance in the next chapter. For now we should find the problem of moral hazard entertaining enough!

The moral hazard problem may be set up formally as follows. Suppose an individual is able to affect the probability of loss by making an expenditure z, such that a higher expenditure achieves a lower probability of loss. This is sometimes referred to as an expenditure on *self-protection*. So p now depends on z and wealth is correspondingly reduced by the amount z. Instead of (7.15) expected utility is now given by,

$$U_m = p(z)u(W - z - x + y - h) + (1 - p(z))u(W - z - h) \quad (7.22)$$

where I assume that $p'(z) < 0$. The individual first chooses the level of expenditure on self-protection, z, and the first-order condition implies that;

$$p'(z^*)[u(W - z^* - x + y - h) - u(W - z^* - h)] =$$
$$p(z^*)u'(W - z^* - x + y - h) + (1 - p(z^*))u'(W - z^* - h) > 0$$
$$(7.23)$$

Since $p'(z) < 0$ it follows that

$$u(W - z^* - h) > u(W - z^* - x + y - h)$$

implying a deductible whatever choice of cover is ultimately made. Moral hazard in this model is represented by the assumption that the premium is unaffected by the level of self-protection. Since the level of z is unobservable to the insurer it follows that the premium cannot be made to depend upon it! Hence,

$$\frac{dh}{dz} = 0 \qquad (7.24)$$

Notice that (7.23) gives z^* as a function of y, a fact which must be borne in mind when carrying out the next step—the choice of cover, y. This choice implies (after some manipulation),

$$p(z)u'(W - z - h - x + y)\left[1 - \frac{dh}{dy}\right] = (1 - p(z))u'(W - z - h)\frac{dh}{dy}$$
$$(7.25)$$

where allowance is made for the dependence of the premium on the level of cover, as in the model of the last section. Hence the demand for insurance depends on the effect of the extent of cover on the premium dh/dy. Since this effect is not determined by the individual but by the insurance company we need to derive an expression for dh/dy from the profit-maximising behaviour of insurers. Further analysis of this model is left as an exercise with some important accompanying reading. More of this is in the Bibliographic guide.

In practice the range of insurance contracts made available is more constrained than the models of this chapter make out. Insurance companies are well aware of moral hazard and its consequences and as far as possible steps are taken to exert moderation in the size of claims and their frequency, and are at great pains, especially with large claims, to establish the circumstances under which losses are incurred. Insurance contracts often specify both the price (the premium) and the quantity (the coverage) on a take-it-or-leave-it basis in order to reduce the temptation of manipulating the assymetric information which pervades these markets. In the absence of safeguards of this type we encounter problems in the existence of equilibrium in insurance markets. An illustration of the issues is presented now.

7.4 EQUILIBRIUM IN A COMPETITIVE INSURANCE MARKET

A competitive equilibrium in this section will have two features. Firstly, the set of all possible equilibrium insurance contracts will earn zero profits for insurance companies (as in the model of the last section). Secondly, there is no insurance contract outside the equilibrium set which makes positive profits. Suppose there are a large number of insurance companies and a large number of potential customers who are all identical in the eyes of the insurers and who may buy only one insurance contract each. For the demanders of insurance, denote their final wealth in the 'no loss' state by W_1 while that in the state with the financial loss by W_2, the expected utility from purchase of cover y at premium h is given by (7.15)

$$U = pu(W - x + y - h) + (1 - p)u(W - h)$$
$$= pu(W_2) + (1 - p)u(W_1) \tag{7.26}$$

where we assume risk-aversion as before.

Suppliers of contracts are risk-neutral and offer all contracts which make positive expected profits. In competitive equilibrium with free entry the expected profit must be zero. Expected profit from each contract is,

$$\bar{\pi} = p(h - y) + (1 - p)h \tag{7.27}$$

which is zero, implying that the premium h is offered at the value of the expected payout—notice there are no overhead costs.

Initially we assume not only that demanders *appear* to be identical to insurance companies but also that they *are* identical, having the same p-values. This presents little problem for the company. An equilibrium contract is one which maximises expected utility for the demander but makes zero profits for firms. The opportunities for demanders are to trade wealth from the 'no loss' state for increased wealth in the 'loss' state by buying insurance cover y.

Each additional unit of cover bought is worth an additional $(1 - p)$ to W_2 and takes p from W_1, this is because $\bar{\pi} = 0$ implies from (7.27) that

$$h = py \tag{7.28}$$

and substituting into W_1 and W_2 shows that

$$W_1 = W - py \tag{7.29}$$

and

$$W_2 = W - x + (1 - p)y$$

so

$$\frac{dW_1}{dy} = -p \quad \text{and} \quad \frac{dW_2}{dy} = (1 - p) \tag{7.30}$$

and hence,

$$\frac{dW_2}{dW_1} = \frac{-(1 - p)}{p} \tag{7.31}$$

In fact (7.31) is the slope of the opportunity constraint facing the individual demander of insurance. This is shown by the line a, E in Figure 7.1. On the other hand along an expected utility indifference curve U we have,

$$\left.\frac{dW_2}{dW_1}\right|_U = -\frac{(1 - p)u'(W_1)}{pu'(W_2)} \tag{7.32}$$

In equilibrium (7.31) and (7.32) are in equality implying

$$u'(W_1) = u'(W_2) \tag{7.33}$$

so that

$$W_1 = W_2 \tag{7.34}$$

or full insurance cover. Equilibrium is given at point E in Figure 7.1. Whereas E is the equilibrium with insurance in this model, a point such as a in Figure 7.1 would be a typical pre-insurance position. Insurer's expected profits may be maintained *and* expected utility of demanders increased by moving from a to E. The line a, E in Figure 7.1 is known as the *fair odds* line, and the 45° ray from the origin represents equal wealth in each state, and since full cover implies equal wealth the equilibrium E lies on the 45° ray.

The position is rather different if demanders have different

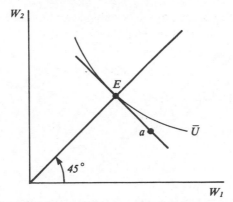

Figure 7.1: Market equilibrium with full insurance cover

probabilities of loss but cannot be identified individually by insuring firms. Suppose that there are just two types of individual who differ only in their p-values. A fraction α of the population are known to have a p-value of p_1 and a fraction $(1 - \alpha)$ a value of p_2 where $p_1 > p_2$. The average probability of loss in the economy as perceived by the insurers is,

$$\bar{p} = \alpha p_1 + (1 - \alpha)p_2 \qquad (7.35)$$

and the fair odds line now has slope $-(1 - \bar{p})/\bar{p}$.

Furthermore (7.26) must be replaced by *two* expected utilities, one for type-1 people and one for type-2 people, U_1 and U_2 respectively, and we find that

$$\left.\frac{dW_2}{dW_1}\right|_{\bar{U}_1} = \frac{(1 - p_1)}{p_1} \frac{u'(W_1)}{u'(W_2)}$$

$$\left.\frac{dW_2}{dW_1}\right|_{\bar{U}_2} = \frac{(1 - p_2)}{p_2} \frac{u'(W_1)}{u'(W_2)}$$

or

$$\left.\frac{dW_2}{dW_1}\right|_{\bar{U}_1} = \frac{p_2}{(1 - p_2)} \frac{(1 - p_1)}{p_1} \left.\frac{dW_2}{dW_1}\right|_{\bar{U}_2} \qquad (7.36)$$

and so the slope of the high-risk indifference curve is a fraction of the slope of the low-risk indifference curve at any level of W_1. Furthermore where the indifference curves intersect and cross the fair odds line the slope of that line must lie between the slope of

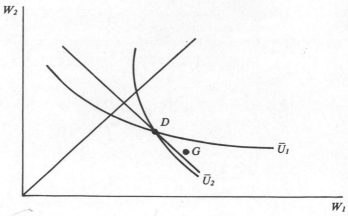

Figure 7.2: Non-existence of 'pooling' equilibrium

U_1 and U_2 (why?). In Figure 7.2 the point D shows an insurance contract (implying a particular distribution of wealth between states) which is offered to both types of individuals. Only one type of contract is offered. Is the contract at D an equilibrium? Well, it is on the fair odds line and so firms are breaking even, so *suppose* D is an equilibrium. Consider the contract at G and suppose this is offered by some companies, then high-risk individuals prefer D and stay with it, but low-risk people prefer G and move to it.

If G is sufficiently close to D the expected profit from supplying the contract G only to low-risk individuals must be very nearly equal to the expected profit from supplying the contract D only to this group. We know that supplying D to all groups gives an expected profit equal to zero, hence supplying D only to low-risk types produces a positive profit, and D cannot be an equilibrium. Denoting the expected profit from contract i as $\bar{\pi}_i(.)$ gives

$$\bar{\pi}_D(\bar{p}) = 0$$
$$\bar{\pi}_D(p_2) > 0$$

therefore

$$\bar{\pi}_G(p_2) \simeq \bar{\pi}_D(p_2) \quad \text{for } G \text{ sufficiently close to } D.$$

Repeated application of this argument to any assumed equilibrium along the fair odds line produces the same result as long as only one type of contract is offered. There is no equilibrium in which different risk classes are offered the same contract. Firms can always increase their profits by producing a contract with marginally different cover and premium which attract only the low-risk individuals. This result is referred to as the non-existence of *pooling equilibrium*.

An equilibrium in a market with different risk classes is possible only if different contracts are offered to different groups in such a way that only high-risk people choose only high-risk contracts and only low-risk people choose only low-risk contracts. An equilibrium which involves self-selection along these lines is known as a *separating equilibrium*.

Explicit recognition of the existence of the two types of individuals by insurance companies causes a segmentation of the market. Instead of one 'average' fair odds line as in Figure 7.2 there are two: one for type-1 people and one for type-2 people. These are the lines (a, c) and (a, d) respectively in Figure 7.3, and because $p_1 > p_2$ the slope of (a, c) is flatter than that of (a, d). Firstly, without much ado, we established equilibrium for the high-risk types of E^H in Figure 7.3. High-risk individuals fully insure.

Now, given the choice, low-risk individuals would also choose full insurance with equilibrium at A. Unfortunately, high-risk individuals would also choose A if it were offered. Therefore *everyone* will buy A. Since everybody has full cover and trade takes

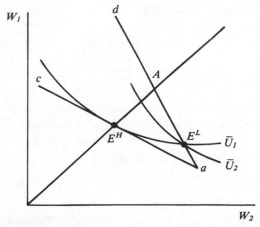

Figure 7.3: Existence of a 'separating' equilibrium

place on the most favourable terms to the consumer profits are
negative, so the contracts E^H and A will not appear together. The
contracts open to low-risk individuals are constrained by the need
to make high-risk individuals stay with E^H. The equilibrium contract for low-risk types which also keeps high-risk types at E^H is E^L
in Figure 7.3.

Hence *if* an equilibrium exists in this market it will be a
separating equilibrium. Unfortunately the existence of even a
separating equilibrium is not guaranteed. In the Bibliographic
guide to this chapter I reveal where a demonstration of this may be
found.

7.5 CONCLUSION

This chapter has examined a variety of issues that arise in markets
for insurance. Such markets exist by and large because although
individuals may face the possibility of incurring large losses an
insuring company with many customers is able to cover against
losses incurred by only a few of them. Insurance companies are
therefore agencies for *spreading* risk.

Some of the key difficulties with insurance markets are that risks
are not easily identifiable and information on the 'quality' of an
insured person is not available to the insuring company. Quality
uncertainty and assymetric information appear in contexts other
than the insurance market and we look at some of these issues in
the following chapter.

7.6 BIBLIOGRAPHIC GUIDE

The demand for insurance by an individual discussed in section 7.2
is based on an exercise in Diamond and Rothschild (1978), which
in turn is based on a paper of Arrow (1963). By and large, the
utility function itself is regarded as being independent of the state.
In the context of medical insurance involving physical injury this
is not an attractive assumption, and in Arrow (1974) this issue is
tackled, and the analysis generalised.

The subject of section 7.3 has been much discussed. The model
presented here draws on that of Pauly (1974) in which self-

protection is modelled as manipulation of the loss probability. The manipulation of the size of loss is often referred to as self-insurance and has been analysed by Spence and Zeckhauser (1971). The reader is also referred to the classic paper by Ehrlich and Becker (1972). Further analysis of the model of equation (7.25) is to be found in Pauly (1974), which the reader is urged to follow up. [See Exercise question 7.3.]

The model of market equilibrium in section 7.4 draws heavily on the paper by Rothschild and Stiglitz (1976) where further details of the non-existence of separating equilibrium are clearly presented.

7.7 EXERCISES

7.1 Show in the context of the 'full-cover' model of section 7.2(a) the effect of an increase in initial wealth on the desired maximum premium.

7.2 Establish the result in (7.21) that in a world where insurance companies cannot observe the accident probability directly more accident prone individuals choose a lower deductible.

7.3 In the model of section 7.3, the optimal choice of insurance cover and of self-protection is presented with the optimal choice of cover determined by equation (7.25). Solve (7.25) for dh/dy and interpret. What policy schedule should be offered by the insurer so that (a) the individual maximises expected utility and (b) the insurer earns zero expected profit? [The policy schedule shows the premium as a function of cover.]

7.4 Why are comprehensive car insurance premiums higher in some central urban areas than in others?

7.5 Why might the separating equilibrium in section 7.4 *not* exist?

7.6 Should people who install burglar alarms pay lower premiums on their house contents insurance?

8. Quality Uncertainty and Signalling

8.1 INTRODUCTION

Problems involving *quality* uncertainty are amongst the most interesting in our subject. The essence of the difficulty is that economic decisions may be made only on the basis of observable characteristics or attributes that are easily ascertained. The price, colour, size and physical specifications of consumer goods and machinery are examples. The appearance and qualifications of a job applicant are others. But these *inspection characteristics* are only helpful if they are associated in some way with the *underlying* qualities that are of ultimate importance. Appearances after all may be deceptive, and often the true value of a commodity or a worker may only be determined after the decision to buy or to hire has taken place. These very important but not readily apparent qualities are known as *experience characteristics*.

Problems arise in markets where important qualities are hidden, possibly until the economic decision to buy, to sell or to hire has been made. In the previous chapter the particular difficulties encountered in insurance markets were discussed. In the next section we examine the problem of adverse selection in a more conventional market where goods are exchanged. In section 8.3 we look at quality uncertainty in the labour market where there may be incentives for able groups to *signal* to prospective employers who otherwise would treat everybody on a low but equal footing.

8.2 THE 'LEMONS' PRINCIPLE

The 'lemons' principle is a consequence of adverse selection, and the name of the principle comes from the American expression for a poor-quality used car. The used-car market is instructive in the discussion of the 'lemons' principle and this section is based largely on a famous example.

In general a difficulty arises in a market where there are 'good' quality used cars and 'poor' quality used cars. Prior to purchase it is very hard for a prospective buyer to know whether a particular car is a good one or a 'lemon'. Consider an individual who buys a brand-new car. Of course even new cars can be 'lemons' although this is less likely, and with warranties it is not so important. After a while the proud owner knows the quality of the car; so suppose it is 'good'. When this car is sold on the second-hand market, however, it is unlikely that it will bring what the seller regards as a 'fair price'. Because the second-hand market is composed of a proportion of poor quality cars, which may be superficially identical to our individual's car, the price which *any* car may trade at is determined by the price at which 'lemons' trade. All superficially similar cars must trade at the same price because cars are indistinguishable from each other, and the price that buyers are willing to pay reflects the expectation on his or her part of buying a lemon. Sadly expectations may be self-fulfilling since the owner of a good car, having reflected on the poor trading prices, may prefer to keep the car until perhaps with age it takes on 'lemon' characteristics. A large proportion of the market are lemons because people expect them to be and the second-hand price is not sufficient to induce the owners of good cars to part with them. In short 'bad cars' drive the 'good cars' out of the market—clearly a problem of adverse selection.

In practice, of course, the situation is more complicated, not least because markets are not simply composed of 'good' and 'bad' quality cars, but rather an almost continuous range of quality of cars with unobservable defects of varying degrees of seriousness. Rather than reducing the adverse selection problem discussed in the binary case, the existence of a range of qualities may make the 'lemons' problem even more acute. To see how, we make use of an example again in the context of a used-car market.

Suppose there are two groups of individuals. Group 1 is the group which starts in possession of cars, while group 2 has no initial endowment of cars. Both groups are expected utility maximisers. Individuals in group 1 buy and sell cars among each other and also sell cars to buyers from group 2. All buyers, whether in group 1 or group 2, do not know the quality of any individual car but are able to estimate the average quality of any cars which appear on the market. As sellers, however, individuals in group 1 do know the quality of each car sold.

Group 1 has utility function

$$u_1 = M + \sum_{i=1}^{n} x_i \qquad (8.1)$$

where M is the consumption of goods other than cars, x_i is the quality of the ith car and n is the number of cars. Group 2 on the other hand has a utility function

$$u_2 = M + \sum_{i=1}^{n} \tfrac{3}{2} x_i \qquad (8.2)$$

Notice that both groups are risk-neutral so that any peculiarities in this market do not arise because of risk-aversion. We need to establish the demand for and supply of cars in the market.

Group 1 has N cars with uniformly distributed quality x where $0 \leq x \leq 2$ and as we have already indicated group 2 has no cars initially. As viewed by all buyers the average quality of all N cars in group 1 is 1. However, since sellers in group 1 may choose which cars to put on the market the average quality of *marketed* cars will depend on the price they bring.

Assume finally that group 1 traders have total income (including that derived from car sales) of y_1 and group 2 an income of y_2. The number of cars N will be taken to be 'large' and indivisibilities are ignored.

(a) *demand for cars by group 1*
   Cars will be demanded by group 1 until the expected marginal utility of cars relative to their price is equal to the marginal utility of other goods relative to their price. Let μ be the expected quality of cars, then μ is also the expected marginal utility of cars because of (8.1); the expected utility of group 1 is

$$u_1 = M + \mu n \qquad (8.3)$$

   The price of cars is p, the marginal utility of other goods 1 and the price of other goods also 1. Hence group 1 will demand cars as long as

$$\frac{\mu}{p} \geq 1 \qquad (8.4)$$

and the number of cars demanded will be y_1/p. The demand for cars by group 1 is therefore

$$D_1 = \begin{cases} y_1/p & \text{if } \mu \geq p \\ 0 & \text{if } \mu < p \end{cases} \qquad (8.5)$$

(b) *supply of cars by group 1*
The price of each extra car sold must compensate group 1 for the loss of utility and, since sellers know the quality of their cars, low prices will only compensate sellers for the loss of low-quality cars. As the price rises higher-quality cars will come on to the market but *all* cars will be put on the market at the same price. When all N cars are put on the market we already know that average quality must be $\mu = 1$ (using the uniform distribution) and the price must compensate for the utility loss from the Nth car, the quality of which is $x_N = 2$, and so $p = 2$ when $\mu = 1$ and N cars are on the market. Similarly when $N/2$ cars are on the market the average quality of car is only $\mu = \frac{1}{2}$ and the loss of utility from $(N/2)^{\text{th}}$ car is $x_{N/2} = 1$, and so $p = 1$ when $\mu = \frac{1}{2}$ and $N/2$ cars are on the market. In general the average quality of cars offered at price p is $p/2$ while the number of cars offered at price p is,

$$S_1 = pN/2 \qquad p \leq 2 \qquad (8.6)$$

(c) *demand for cars by group 2*
In an analogous way to the method under (a) we have

$$D_2 = \begin{cases} y_2/p & \text{if } 3\mu/2 \geq p \\ 0 & \text{if } 3\mu/2 < p \end{cases} \qquad (8.7)$$

(d) *supply of cars by group 2*
Obviously, since group 2 have no cars,

$$S_2 = 0$$

Aggregate demand and supply in this market are summarised in Table 8.1.

All is not well however because at any price p, the average quality of cars in the market is $p/2$, and substitution of this value for μ into the first column of Table 8.1 reveals that the only possible range of prices is the last one, $3\mu/2 < p$. No cars are demanded here and therefore there is no market for cars.

Table 8.1: Demand and supply of automobiles

Range of p	D_1	D_2	D	S
$0 < p \leqq \mu$	y_1/p	y_2/p	$(y_1 + y_2)/p$	$pN/2$
$\mu < p \leqq \frac{3}{2}\mu$	0	y_2/p	y_2/p	$pN/2$
$\frac{3}{2}\mu < p$	0	0	0	$pN/2$

Market price depends on average quality *and* average quality depends on price. At a high price many cars are forthcoming and the average quality is high. However, there is an excess of supply for cars, which warrants a price fall. As a result the better cars are withdrawn from the market and average quality falls. The marginal utility of cars falls and the price people are willing to pay falls further and so on. In the words of Akerlof—a pioneer of analyses but of this type—we have not merely the bad cars driving out good cars

> bad driving out the not-so-bad driving out the medium driving out the not-so-good driving out the good.
> [Akerlof (1970)]

One ingredient missing from the analysis is that of 'certification'. It may pay the owner of a good car to acquire a certificate indicating the fact. It may also pay the owner of a 'lemon' to acquire some illicit certification also. Hence, for certification to be useful it must make the acquisition of a certificate worthwhile for the high-quality types and not worthwhile for the low-quality types. We consider a model in this vein now.

8.3　THE ECONOMICS OF SIGNALLING

Rather than pursue a product market example, we follow the early literature by considering quality uncertainty in the labour market. Furthermore, since the standard reference on this is highly readable I will merely give the ingredients of the basic model.

Consider a single labour market composed of a number of workers of different productivities. For simplicity there are just two productivities 1 and 2, and hence two types of worker, with type 1 (with marginal product of 1) forming a proportion $q(< 1)$ of the labour force. Since there are just two types of worker, the remaining workers are type 2 (with marginal product of 2) forming a proportion $(1 - q)$ of the labour force.

In the absence of any *screening* of job applicants by firms and of any *signalling* by workers, all workers will be regarded as being identical by employers. Furthermore the wage offered by firms will be the average marginal product of workers $q + 2(1 - q)$ or $2 - q$.

Suppose that workers of both types are able to buy a certificate stating their education level and that any amount of education may be bought—at a cost. It is assumed that the amount of education y is a continuous variable (measured for example in terms of time spent in full-time education) and via the certificate is an observable and reliable signal. Education costs type-1 workers twice as much as it costs type-2 workers. The costs are

$$c_1 = y \tag{8.8}$$

and

$$c_2 = y/2 \tag{8.9}$$

With the presence of education as a signal, employees will form beliefs about the level of education acquired by each group. Suppose these beliefs are such that productivity is perfectly correlated with education. Given the costs in (8.8) and (8.9) the correlation will be positive with the high-productivity group acquiring more education than the low-productivity group. We have an equilibrium in this market only if the employers' beliefs are confirmed by the education choices of each group. In our specific example we assume that there is a level of education y^* such that employers believe that all workers with $y < y^*$ are low-productivity workers and those with $y \geq y^*$ are high-productivity workers. Having confidence in these beliefs the employer will accordingly set a wage equal to 1 (the marginal product of type-1 workers) for workers with $y < y^*$ and a wage equal to 2 (the marginal product of type-2 workers) for workers with $y \geq y^*$.

An example of a wage structure of this type along with the cost curves of (8.8) and (8.9) is shown in Figure 8.1. The question at issue is whether this announced wage structure provides the appropriate incentives for individuals to acquire the amount of education

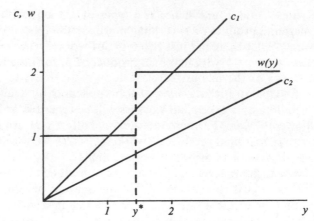

Figure 8.1: Signalling equilibrium

which will ultimately confirm the initial beliefs of employers. It is apparent that the net benefit from acquiring education for group 1, $w(y) - c_1$ is maximised at $y = 0$ and no education is acquired. For group 2 on the other hand the net benefit $w(y) - c_2$ is maximised at $y = y^*$. Hence all workers of type 1 will have no education and will receive $w(0) = 1$ while those of type 2 will have y^* education and will receive $w(y^*) = 2$. The initial beliefs of employers will be confirmed. It is equally apparent that any value of y^* between 1 and 2 would have produced an equilibrium of this kind. Therefore there are an infinity of equilibria.

The welfare properties of these equilibria are worth considering. Type-1 workers are indifferent between the very many values which y may take between 1 and 2 since no education costs will be incurred. Type-2 workers, however, are worse off as y^* moves away from 1 and towards 2 since their surplus from acquiring education is being eroded.

Finally, it is interesting to ask whether the equilibrium without signalling is preferred to or is inferior to the signalling equilibrium. Type-1 workers would receive the average wage of $2 - q$ in the absence of signalling and would receive a wage of 1 with signalling. Thus, since $2 - q > 1$, type-1 workers prefer the no-signalling market. It is left as an exercise to establish how workers of type 2 feel between the no-signalling and signalling equilibrium.

One important distinction that has been made in the literature is between *signals* which are acquired characteristics of an individuals and *indices* which are individual characteristics which cannot be changed. Colour and sex are examples of indices, whereas educational attainment, discussed in this section, would generally be thought of as a signal. This distinction is important, not least because of the interplay between indices and acquired characteristics. It is possible that poor indices ('poor' in the eyes of employers) must be counterbalanced by overinvestment in a signal. We do not pursue this formally here but references in the Bibliographic guide should be followed up.

8.4 CONCLUSION

In this short chapter we have explored two models of quality uncertainty. The non-existence in a market with adverse selection was discussed in section 8.2 and highlighted some of the problems introduced initially in Chapter 7. In section 8.3 a model was introduced to explain the role of signals in helping to distinguish between high- and low-productivity workers.

One interesting topic not discussed explicitly here is the screening of applicants by firms. In the model of the previous section we may interpret y^* chosen by employers as a 'screen', in the sense that it is this which enables employers to discriminate. There are in practice many screening devices which may go beyond individual's signals. It is likely in practice that for 'high-quality' jobs an application quoting educational achievements may be only the first step in being accepted. Interviews, further examination and even short courses are further 'screens' set up by employers. The investment by firms in screening devices is therefore the market partner of investment in signals by workers.

8.5 BIBLIOGRAPHIC GUIDE

The standard reference on the 'lemons' problem is Akerlof (1970) and that on signalling is Spence (1973). Readers interested in following up a general discussion on screening and signalling in the labour market are referred to Joll *et al.* (1983). Some exercises, in addition to those which follow, may be found in Diamond and Rothschild (1978) and in de Meza and Osborne (1980).

8.6 EXERCISES

8.1 Why do one-month-old cars sell for less than brand-new cars?

8.2 Why might the social rate of return to education differ from the private rate of return? What are the consequences of this for the amount of education people acquire?

8.3 Suppose there are three groups of individuals of differing productivity and who are able to acquire education at differing costs. Assume that high-productivity workers may acquire education at lower cost. Construct a model similar to that of section 8.3. Suppose initially that firms are unable to distinguish between the achievements of the highest two productivity groups and in fact holds initial belief that there are just two groups. What will happen? What will an equilibrium, if it exists, look like?

8.4 Suppose there are two types of individual in the economy (as in the model of section 8.3) but two markets, one which pays according to educational attainment and one which does not. Set up a problem along these lines. What determines the distribution of employment between the two markets?

8.5 Using the model of section 8.3 we established that type-1 workers prefer the situation with no signalling. Which situation do type-2 workers prefer? What do you conclude about the overall welfare benefits of signalling?

9. Searching for Information

9.1 INTRODUCTION

Almost exclusively we have considered decision-making in a *static* setting. By static in this context I mean that individuals have responded to uncertainty in a passive way and have had no opportunity of improving their information about alternatives before reaching a final choice. In this chapter we consider briefly a number of issues which arise when individuals actively seek to improve their knowledge about market opportunities. We do this in the context of so-called *search theory*. This quite general set of techniques has a large number of applications, not only in economics. The specific problems we examine in this chapter are, firstly the consumer searching for low prices, and secondly a worker searching for 'good' jobs. In the next section we outline the ingredients of search problems in general and some of the broad issues raised.

9.2 SEARCH MODELS

Search is simply a term used to describe *any* information-gathering exercise. The benefits to be expected from this activity are contained in the varied opportunities which may be unearthed as a result of 'shopping around'. On the other hand, enquiries, even the most casual, may involve a cost if not in cash terms then in terms of inconvenience and general utility loss. Expressed in this way it is clear that search activity may be formulated in a way which underlies all economic decisions involving a balance of costs and benefits.

The precise way in which a search model is formulated depends on exactly how the search process is carried out. A moment's thought brings to mind a variety of ways in which information may be sought and a variety of circumstances in which search may be appropriate. Some examples are searching for a bargain or discount, for a better quality home computer or for a higher-paying job. Information may be gathered in a variety of ways: visiting stores randomly, or visiting stores selected from a newspaper, selecting reputable brand names from a consumer magazine or specialist magazine, and so on. Before we consider any of the well-known contributions to search theory, which require us to acquire some new techniques, consider the following problem, which may be solved using techniques developed earlier in the book.

A consumer wishes to buy just one unit of a good which is normally priced at p per unit. However, a certain proportion of the local stores offer a discount of ρ on each unit. The consumer *knows* that a proportion q of stores offer no discount while a proportion $(1 - q)$ do offer a discount. However, I assume that the consumer *does not know* exactly which stores are offering the discount. Clearly if the consumer did know this there would be no search problem because the consumer could approach the discount store directly. As usual, utility is given by the increasing and concave function $u(.)$. I assume that the individual consumer wants the good sufficiently to have at least one attempt at a purchase, and that there is a cost of c involved in visiting a store regardless of how successful that visit is. Furthermore I assume, for expositional convenience, that utility is separable in search cost and product price, and each visit imposes a disutility of $u(-c) < 0$. There appear to be three possible outcomes resulting from a visit. Firstly, there may be no purchase, in which case the disutility $u(-c)$ is incurred. Secondly, the consumer may buy the good priced at p with no discount, in which case total utility is $u(-c) + u(-p)$ where $u(-p) > 0$ because of the utility derived from having the good. Finally, the consumer may buy the good at discount and receive total utility $u(-c) + u(-p + \rho)$. It seems reasonable that

$$u(-p) < u(-p + \rho) \tag{9.1}$$

I now give the consumer a choice between two alternatives. *Either*, visit one store and buy one unit of the good regardless of whether a discount is available or not, *or* visit one store and buy the good only if a discount is offered and try another store if not—however, only one more store is tried and a purchase made there at full price or at discount depending on what is offered. Notice that with the second alternative a consumer who is unsuccessful on the first attempt *buys* a second attempt. For simplicity only one additional attempt is permitted. Clearly, the second alternative involves a limited amount of search whereas the first alternative contains no search element. Now, an expected utility maximiser chooses that alternative which has the greater expected utility. The expected utility from the first alternative is

$$U_1 = u(-c) + qu(-p) + (1-q)u(-p+\rho) \qquad (9.2)$$

while that from the second alternative is

$$U_2 = u(-c) + (1-q)u(-p+\rho) + \\ q\{u(-c) + qu(-p) + (1-q)u(-p+\rho)\} \qquad (9.3)$$

The expected utility from the first alternative necessarily involves a disutility of calling at the store plus the expected utility from the purchase. The expected utility of the second alternative involves the disutility of calling at the first store plus the expected utility if a discount is found. If no discount is found (with probability q) the consumer goes on to the next store, again incurring the disutility, but this time making the purchase for certain with expected utility $qu(-p) + (1-q)u(-p+\rho)$.

With p, ρ and q fixed, it is clear that the relative attractiveness of the two alternatives is determined by the search cost. First, we equate (9.2) and (9.3) to find the expression implied by indifference between the two options. This turns out to be

$$(1-q)u(-p) = u(-c) + (1-q)u(-p+\rho) \qquad (9.4)$$

Let the value of c solving (9.4) be c_0. It is easily shown that U_1 is greater than U_2 (the first alternative is preferred to the second) if

$$(1-q)u(-p) > u(-c) + (1-q)u(-p+\rho) \qquad (9.5)$$

while U_1 is less than U_2 (the second alternative is preferred) if

$$(1-q)u(-p) < u(-c) + (1-q)u(-p+\rho) \qquad (9.6)$$

Now (9.5) differs from (9.4) in that the right-hand side has fallen, which implies (given p, ρ and q) a change in c. In fact the required change in c is one which makes $u(-c)$ more negative and greater disutility is clearly associated with increased search cost. Hence $U_1 > U_2$ is associated with $c > c_0$. It is easily established that (9.6) implies that $U_1 < U_2$ is associated with $c < c_0$. The relationships between U_1, U_2 and c are illustrated in Figure 9.1. It is easily

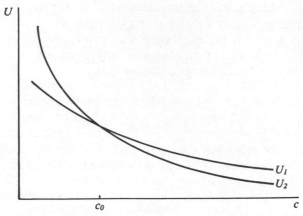

Figure 9.1: Search and search costs

verified, using calculus on (9.2) and (9.3), that U_2 has a steeper slope than U_1 at each value of c.

It is clear now that search will be preferred if the search cost c is relatively low ($U_2 > U_1$) whereas the consumer simply buys from the first shop if the search cost is relatively high ($U_1 > U_2$). As we shall see this result is almost universal in search theory. *The amount of search falls as search costs rise.* Here, we have constrained things so that the choice is merely between 'search' (a second store) or 'do not search'. The issue of *how much* search to undertake is dealt with presently.

Before we leave this simple model, it is interesting to observe the effect of an increase in the discount ρ on the choice between the alternatives. An increase in ρ in terms of Figure 9.1 increases both U_1 and U_2 for each c, but has a greater effect on U_2 than on U_1. It can be established, using (9.4), that the effect of these shifts is to increase c_0 (the calculations are left as an exercise). The implication is that an increase in the discount increase the benefit of search and raises the threshold search cost at which search ceases to be the preferred alternative.

9.3 GATHERING PRICE INFORMATION

The model of the previous section, though useful as an introduction to the idea of search, suffers from having an arbitrary amount of search taking place, the emphasis being on whether or not it is worthwhile visiting two stores rather than just one in the hope of finding a discount. In this section we consider not only whether search is worthwhile or not but also *how much* search is worthwhile. Thus, in the initial specification of the model we leave open-ended the number of shops to be visited before a purchase is made—hopefully this will be determined by the model.

Suppose that there are a large number of shops offering a range of prices for a particular product. As in the previous section the consumer wants to buy just one unit of the product. Suppose further that the prices available are known to be 10, 20 and 30 and are distributed among shops in the proportions ¼, ½ and ¼ respectively. That is, it is known that one-quarter of the stores offer the good at 10, one-half at 20 and a further one-quarter offer the good at 30. Now, the consumer would prefer to buy the good at the lowest price 10, but *expects* to pay a price of 20 if only one store is visited because,

$$E[p] = \frac{1}{4}(10) + \frac{1}{2}(20) + \frac{1}{4}(30) = 20 \qquad (9.7)$$

Could our consumer do any better than this by visiting a few more stores and gathering more price information? After all, *some* shops are offering the good at half of the expected price! On the benefit side alone the answer is clearly, yes. However, whether it is worth gathering extra price information depends not only on the benefit of expected price reduction but also on the cost of additional search. These are the ingredients of our problem. To see how they work out, we consider first the benefit of search. The consumer is allowed to visit any desired number of stores, although (anticipating the costs involved) the fewer stores the better. The individual will observe the price at each store until the desired number (determined before leaving home) have been collected. The consumer then has a sample of, say, n prices and chooses the lowest price in the sample, say p^*, by returning to the store (or one of the stores) which offered p^*. However, since the number of visits to be made is determined before search commences the consumer is unable to establish exactly what the lowest price to be observed in a given sample will be, because this depends on the 'luck of the draw'. Rather, the consumer calculates the *expected* minimum price to be found in a sample of a given size. Intuitively, the larger the sample of prices collected the greater is the expectation that the sample contains the lowest available price, and the smaller is the *expected minimum price*. That this is so may be verified formally, but for now the point may be illustrated by continuing with our example. We need to identify for each conceivable sample size, from 1 upwards, the quantity described as the 'expected minimum price' of the sample, say $E[p_n^*]$, where $n = 1, 2, \ldots$ With a large number of stores the sample size may be very large (until it accounts for all the stores), although it is unlikely that a very large number of price quotes will be necessary.

(i)   *determining $E[p_1^*]$*
      Consider all possible samples of size $n = 1$; there are just three, but to establish a routine that will help later we construct a table. Table 9.1 shows the possible samples (column 1), the probability of the sample (column 2) and the sample minimum (column 3). The fourth column shows the product of each sample minimum with the sample probability and the sum of the items in column 4 is the expected minimum price from a sample of 1. Notice that $E[p_1^*] = E[p]$.

(ii) *determining $E[p_2^*]$*
      A similar procedure underlies the derivation of $E[p_2^*]$ and is summarised in Table 9.2. This time all the samples of size $n = 2$ are listed in column 1. Notice now that $E[p_2^*] < E[p_1^*]$, confirming that there are expected price savings from increasing the sample size from $n = 1$ to $n = 2$.

(iii) *determining $E[p_3^*]$*
      What about $n = 3$? A full summary of the calculation is

Table 9.1: Calculation of $E[p_1^*]$

(1) Sample	(2) Probability of sample	(3) Minimum of sample	(2) × (3)
(10)	¼	10	2.5
(20)	½	20	10.0
(30)	¼	30	7.5
			$E[p_1^*] = 20.0$

Table 9.2: Calculation of $E[p_2^*]$

(1) Sample	(2) Probability of sample	(3) Minimum of sample	(2) × (3)
(10, 10)	1/16	10	10/16
(10, 30)	1/16	10	10/16
(10, 20)	2/16	10	20/16
(20, 10)	2/16	10	20/16
(20, 20)	4/16	20	80/16
(20, 30)	2/16	20	40/16
(30, 20)	2/16	20	40/16
(30, 10)	1/16	10	10/16
(30, 30)	1/16	30	30/16

$$E[p_2^*] = 16.25$$

rather tedious and is omitted here, however, readers may verify that $E[p_3^*] = 14.38$.

We may proceed in this way indefinitely, but for our purposes we need go no higher than $E[p_4^*] = 13.20$. Before considering the associated costs of search it is worth considering the interpretation to be placed on the quantity.

$$\Delta_{n+1} = E[p_n^*] - E[p_{n+1}^*] \qquad (9.8)$$

We will refer to Δ_{n+1} as the expected price reduction from increasing the sample size from n to $n + 1$, as such (9.8) is the incremental expected saving from additional search or the additional value from searching $n + 1$ times rather than only n times. The appropriate values of $E[p_n^*]$ and Δ_{n+1} are shown in columns 2 and 3 of Table 9.3. For example, we conclude that increasing the sample from $n = 2$ to $n = 3$ brings an expected price reduction (that is, an expected saving) of 1.87. Notice that while increasing the sample size continually produces expected savings the successive expected price reductions become smaller. It will not come as a surprise to learn that the numbers in the third column approach zero and those in the second column approach 10.00 as n increases indefinitely to include the entire 'population' of stores. Notice also that, as with many 'expected values' encountered in the book, the figures in column 2 of Table 9.3 do not indicate prices that will actually be

Table 9.3: Sample size and expected price reduction

(1) n	(2) $E[p_n^*]$	(3) $\Delta n + 1$
1	20.00	—
2	16.25	3.75
3	14.38	1.87
4	13.20	1.18

found—these may only take values 10, 20 and 30—but are merely representative of the improved prospects which accompany increases in sample size.

Now for the costs. As before I assume that *each* visit to a store involves a fixed, known cost, c. Thus, if n stores are visited the total cost is cn, while the *additional* cost incurred in visiting $n + 1$ stores rather than n is simply $c(n + 1) - cn = c$. Clearly it will not pay the consumer to search the $(n + 1)$th time if the expected saving from so doing is less than the extra cost.

Hence, suppose $c = 1.50$, then referring to Table 9.3 we see that a sample size of 3 is worthwhile whereas a sample size of 4 is not. The cost of increasing the sample from 3 to 4 is 1.50, while the expected saving is only 1.18. Alternatively, suppose that $c = 3.50$, then by similar reasoning a sample size of 2 is worthwhile whereas a sample size of 3 is not. We conclude then that,

the amount of search falls as the cost of search increases.

Moving away from the particular example a more general summary of the problem is presented in Figure 9.2. Frame (a) gives the total cost and expected minimum price associated with each sample size, n, while frame (b) shows the associated marginal curves. The form of the expected minimum price curve is quite general while the cost curve depends on the assumption of constant unit search costs. Using frame (b) in Figure 9.2 it is clear that an increase in c lowers the amount of search.

This concludes the analysis of this simple model of information-gathering. However, there are two points worth mentioning now. Firstly, the analysis of this section has not been formulated in terms of expected utility maximising behaviour but rather in terms of

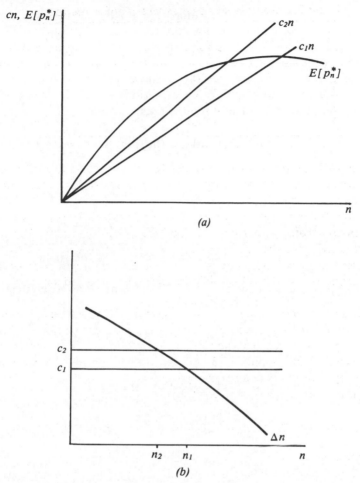

Figure 9.2: Returns to search

cost-minimisation. This is really a matter of expositional convenience and at least in principle the analysis in terms of expected
utility may be solved with analogous results. The second point is
rather more substantial and results from an apparent weakness of
the search process itself. Recall that the sample size is chosen prior
to search commencing—in line with the marginal cost and benefit
considerations of Figure 9.2. Hence, suppose we find that $n = 4$ is
recommended by our calculations, then strictly speaking we should

search four stores only—no more and no less. Thus even if we encounter a price of 10 on our third try we should still carry on to search a fourth store. This is clearly wasteful, but is perfectly consistent with the rational behaviour of the cost—benefit calculus because our calculations of $E[p_n^*]$ allow for *all* possible samples including those with multiple observations of 10! It would seem more sensible to substitute for the present rule

> search n stores and choose the minimum price of the n received.

with

> search at most n stores and stop search as soon as lowest price is encountered or stop after n stores and choose the minimum price of the n received, whichever occurs the sooner.

Happily the need for this second, somewhat more complicated, rule is avoided by the following

> select a reservation price p_r and buy at first store which asks for a price no greater than p_r.

This is referred to as a reservation price rule and avoids the problem of selecting as fixed sample by considering the acceptability of each price as it is observed in the (random) sequence. This rule takes advantage of opportunities presented by the early (fortuitous) observation of a low price.

Rather than consider this *sequential* search problem in the context of a search for low prices, I will move on to an application of search which has proved to be one of the most fruitful.

9.4   A SIMPLE MODEL OF SEQUENTIAL JOB SEARCH

Consider the following problem facing the unemployed job-searcher. There are a large number of possible jobs for which the worker is qualified and they offer a variety of wages. Ideally, the worker would prefer the highest-paid job available but, unfortunately, does not know where this may be found. In a way similar to our consumer of the last section the worker may know the *distribution* of wage offers but not where each wage offer is located. (We leave aside, for the moment, the question of whether this situation is one which faces a significant number of workers and concentrate on the mathematical structure of the problem.) Rather than re-run the search procedure of the previous section we will allow the worker-searcher to set about the task in a somewhat different way. Suppose that, prior to any search taking place, the worker chooses, on the basis of expected costs and benefits, a wage called the *reservation wage* such that once search starts all wage offers (received in random order) falling below the reservation wage are rejected while the first wage encountered which is not less than the reservation wage is accepted. The central role is clearly played by the reservation wage which essentially separates those wages which are acceptable (those greater than the reservation wage) from those which are not acceptable (those less thatn the reservation wage). Hence this problem is solved for the searcher once the reservation wage is determined and I now show how it is done.

I will continue with the example of the previous section, except that the 'prices' (10, 20, and 30) are now to be regarded as *wages*. The wages available to the searcher are therefore known to be distributed in the following way:

$$\left.\begin{array}{l} Pr[W = 10] = 0.25 \\ Pr[W = 20] = 0.50 \\ Pr[W = 30] = 0.25 \end{array}\right\} \qquad (9.9)$$

In the previous section we calculated the desired amount of search by calculating the expected marginal benefit and marginal cost for each possible amount of search ($n = 1, 2, \ldots$) and choosing that amount of search which equated (as nearly as possible) the marginal costs and benefits. This is a very common procedure in economics and is equivalent to maximising the return to search *net* of search costs. However, in sequential search we do not choose the amount of search directly since how much search actually takes place depends on how lucky we are in finding an acceptable offer. Because the appropriate 'marginal conditions' are not so obvious under sequential search we calculate the expected net return to search for each possible reservation wage and then select that reservation wage which maximises expected net return. Let $V(r)$ be defined as the total expected net return to searching once more when the reservation wage is r. In our example, r may take the values 10, 20 and 30, however for the moment we leave the precise value unspecified so that we may derive a quite general formula for $V(r)$. In fact the formula is easily derived if we remember that, by the definition of the reservation wage, r those wage offers which fall short of r will be rejected and search will continue. The formula for $V(r)$ is;

$$V(r) = E[W|W \geq r]Pr[W \geq r] + V(r)Pr[W < r] - c \qquad (9.10)$$

Interpreting the right-hand side of (9.10) we have, firstly, that if an offer is accepted, the expected return is the (conditional) expected value of W given that $W \geq r$, an event with probability $Pr[W \geq r]$. Clearly before search starts we know only that an accepted offer is going to be greater than or equal to r but we do not know exactly which offer it will be. Hence the *expected acceptable offer* is the expected value of W *conditional* on $W \geq r$, $E[W|W \geq r]$ we turn to the calculation of this quantity presently. The second term on the right-hand side of (9.10) is the return to search multiplied by the probability that a wage falls short of r. In this case search does not end but continues with return $V(r)$ by definition. The final term is the search cost, which is deducted whether or not the current search is successful.

Noting that $Pr[W < r] = \{1 - Pr[W \geq r]\}$ we may solve (9.10) for $V(r)$ to give the equation

$$V(r) = E[W|W \geq r] - \frac{c}{Pr[W \geq r]} \qquad (9.11)$$

which is to be maximised by choosing r. The appropriate caculations using our example and assuming that $c = 5$ are summarised in Table 9.4. Notice that,

$$Pr[W \geq r] = \sum_{W \geq r} Pr[W] \qquad (9.12)$$

and

$$E[W|W \geq r] = \frac{\sum_{W \geq r} WPr[W]}{\sum_{W \geq r} Pr[W]} \qquad (9.13)$$

The calculation of the first row of Table 9.4 is as follows. Assuming $r = 10$, we have

$$E[W \mid W \geq r] = \frac{10(0.25) + 20(0.5) + 30(0.25)}{0.25 + 0.5 + 0.25}$$

$$= 20.00$$

and

$$Pr[W \geq r] = 0.25 + 0.5 + 0.25 = 1.00.$$

The other rows are similarly calculated using (9.12) and (9.13).

It is easily seen from Table 9.4 that $V(r)$ is greatest when $r = 20.00$. The searcher will accept the first wage received which is 20.00 or more and reject the wage of 10.00 always. However, the question of how much search will take place has not been answered and cannot be answered for certain. To help us find an answer to this, return to equation (9.11), the first term of which is the expected benefit of search and the second term the expected cost. This latter may be thought of as being the product of two terms, the search cost, c, and the expected number of times the search cost must be paid, $1/Pr[W \geq r]$. Hence $1/Pr[W \geq r]$ has the interpretation of being the expected number of searches. The formal demonstration of this is outside the scope of this book, but we see that if $r = 20.00$ the expected number of searches is 4/3. This seems reasonable. If we use a reservation wage of 20.00, only wage offers of 10.00, constituting only a quarter of all wages, will be rejected and we would not expect to require lengthy search before a wage offer of 20.00 or of 30.00 is received. In fact, one or two searches seems about right.

As with the model of the previous section we are able to establish that increases in the search cost will tend to lower the (expected) amount of search; however, in this sequential model it does so by lowering the reservation wage. A reworking of the example with $c = 12.00$ establishes that r falls from 20.00 to 10.00.

Table 9.4: Reservation wages and returns to search

r	$E[w \mid \geq r]$	$c/Pr[W \geq r]$	$V(r)$
10	20.00	5.00	15.00
20	23.33	6.67	16.66
30	30.00	20.00	10.00

The results of the sequential search model and its overall structure are more general than our example suggests. For completeness I now turn briefly to a more general formulation of the problem, which has the advantage of being amenable to calculus so that the 'marginal condition' of the sequential model may be expressed explicitly.

9.5 THE CALCULUS OF SEQUENTIAL JOB SEARCH

Suppose that there are a large number of wage offers with a distribution $f(W)$, for $0 < W < \infty$, then using the definition of the previous section we have,

$$V(r) = \int_r^\infty Wf(W)\,\mathrm{d}W + V(r)\int_0^r f(W)\,\mathrm{d}W - c \qquad (9.14)$$

From which, solving for $V(r)$ and noting that $\int_0^r f(W)\,\mathrm{d}W = F(r)$ we have

$$V(r) = \left\{\int_r^\infty Wf(W)\,\mathrm{d}W - c\right\}\Big/[1 - F(r)] \qquad (9.15)$$

which corresponds to (9.11). Differentiating (9.15) with respect to r gives

$$V'(r) = \left[-rf(r)[1 - F(r)] + f(r)\left\{\int_r^\infty Wf(W)\,\mathrm{d}W - c\right\}\right]\Big/[1 - F(r)]^2$$

$$(9.16)$$

and setting (9.16) equal to zero implies that $V(r)$ achieves a maximum when

$$0 = \int_{r^*}^\infty (W - r^*)f(W)\,\mathrm{d}W - c \qquad (9.17)$$

or,

$$c = \int_{r^*}^\infty (W - r^*)f(W)\,\mathrm{d}W \qquad (9.18)$$

which is a very famous result in search theory, the right-hand side representing the expected gain from additional search. Two implications for this are easily derived. Firstly, substituting (9.18) into (9.15) and thus eliminating c gives

$$V(r^*) = r^* \qquad (9.19)$$

which states that the optimal reservation wage r^* makes the searcher indifferent between accepting precisely r^* and continuing search receiving $V(r^*)$. Secondly, a comparative-static exercise on (9.18) reveals that

$$\frac{dr^*}{dc} = -1/[1 - F(r^*)] < 0 \qquad (9.20)$$

thus confirming that an increase in the search cost lowers the reservation wage.

9.6 CONCLUSION

Hopefully this chapter has given a flavour of the structure of simple search models. The literature on search theory is now immense and a wide variety of job search models in particular are available. This arises because of the very many different assumptions which can be made about the market environment. For example, suppose not all firms approached have vacancies, or suppose that the searcher is not unemployed but is seeking wage improvement above the current wage received. The possibilities are limitless but most have now received attention in the literature. Unfortunately, we are unable to pursue the implications of these apparently more realistic models here.

9.7 BIBLIOGRAPHIC GUIDE

A general introduction to consumer and job search models may be found in Hey (1979). A comprehensive analysis of various job search models is available in McKenna (1985), while an interesting collection of original papers is contained in Lippman and McCall (1979).

9.8 EXERCISES

9.1 (a) Use calculus to verify that U_1 and U_2 in section 9.2 are related in the way depicted in Figure 9.1.
      (b) Hence verify the claim in the text that an increase in the discount increases c_0, and discuss this result.

9.2   Set up and solve a sequential model of consumer search for the lowest price. Demonstrate that an increase in the search cost raises the reservation price.

9.3   In the model of sequential job search, suppose that a wage offer is received on each search only with probability q (rather than with certainty as in the text), and with probability $(1 - q)$ of no wage offer. Set up and solve this model. Determine the effect of an increase in q on the reservation wage. Interpret the role played by q.

9.4   Continuing with the model in the previous question, suppose that with probability q a wage offer is received and with probability $(1 - q)$ the job searcher receives unemployment benefit u_0. Determine the effect of an increase in u_0 on the reservation wage. [Adventurous students may attempt to determine the effect of an increase in unemployment benefit on the duration of unemployment in this model.]

Conclusion

This book has covered a wide variety of topics in the economics of uncertainty, but many gaps remain. Some of these will have been filled by attempts at the exercises and a perusal of the further reading. It is to be hoped that many readers will have found this book a sound starting point for a programme of study which is both insightful and rewarding.

Many current issues of both a theoretical and practical nature are being approached using some type of uncertainty framework. A glance at recent issues of leading journals is evidence of that. However, so widespread is uncertainty and so crucial a role does it play in both individual decisions and market outcomes that its revelance in economic studies is likely to be long-lasting.

References

Akerlof, G. (1970) 'The market for 'lemons': qualitative uncertainty and the price mechanism', *Quarterly Journal of Economics*, **84**, 488–500.

Allais, M. (1953) 'Le comportement de l'homme rationnel devant le risque: critique des postulates et axiomes de l'école Americaine', *Econometrica*, October, 503–46.

Arrow, K. J. (1951) 'Alternative approaches to the theory of choice in risk-taking situations', *Econometrica*, **19**, 404–37.

—— (1959) 'Toward a theory of price adjustment', in Abramovitz, M. *et al.*, *The Allocation of Economic Resources*, Stanford University Press, Stanford, 41–51.

—— (1963) 'Uncertainty and the welfare economics of medical care', *American Economic Review*, **53**, 941–69. Also in Diamond and Rothschild (1978).

—— (1965) *Some Aspects of the Theory of Risk Bearing*, Yrjö Jahnssonin säätiö, Helsinki.

—— (1974) 'Optimal insurance and generalized deductibles', *Scandinavian Actuarial Journal*, 1–42.

Deaton, A. and Muellbauer, J. (1980) *Economics and Consumer Behaviour*, Cambridge University Press, Cambridge.

DeGroot, M. H. (1970) *Optimal Statistical Decisions*, McGraw-Hill, New York.

de Meza, D. and Osborne, M. (1980), *Exercises in Price Theory*, Philip Allan, Oxford.

Diamond, P. A. (1967) 'The role of the stock market in a general equilibrium model with technological uncertainty', *American Economic Review*, **57**, 759–73. Also in Diamond and Rothschild (1978).

Diamond, P. A. and Rothschild, M. (1978) *Uncertainty in Economics: Readings and Exercises*, Academic Press, New York.

Ehrlich, I. and Becker, G. S. (1972) 'Market insurance, self-insurance and self-protection', *Journal of Political Economy*, **82**(2), March, 623–48.

Ford, J. L. (1983) *Choice, Expectation and Uncertainty*, Martin Robertson, Oxford.

Goodhart, C. A. E. (1975) *Money, Information and Uncertainty*, MacMillan, London.

Gravelle, H. and Rees, R. (1981) *Microeconomics*, Longman, London.

Green, H. A. J. (1971) *Consumer Theory*, MacMillan, London.

Henderson, J. M. and Quandt, R. E. (1980), *Microeconomic Theory*, McGraw-Hill, New York.

Hey, J. D. (1979) *Uncertainty in Microeconomics*, Martin Robertson, Oxford.

—— (1981) *Economics in Disequilibrium*, Martin Robertson, Oxford.

Joll, C. *et al.* (1983) *Developments in Labour Market Analysis*, George Allen and Unwin, London.

Kahneman, D. and Tversky, A. (1979) 'Prospect theory: an analysis of decisions under risk', *Econometrica*, **47**(2), March, 263–91.

Laidler, D. (1981) *An Introduction to Microeconomics*, Philip Allan, Oxford (2nd edn.).

Layard, R. and Walters, A. (1978) *Microeconomic theory*, McGraw-Hill, Maidenhead.

Lippman, S. A. and McCall, J. J. (eds.) (1979) *Studies in the Economics of Search*, North-Holland, Amsterdam.

Lippman, S. A. and McCall, J. J. (1981) 'The economics of uncertainty: selected topics and probabilistic methods', in Arrow, K. J. and Intriligator, M. D. (eds.) *Handbook of Mathematical Economics*, Vol. 1, North-Holland, Amsterdam.

Loomes, G. and Sugden, R. (1982) 'Regret theory: an alternative theory of rational choice under uncertainty', *Economic Journal*, **92** (368), December, 805–24.

Luce, R. D. and Raiffa, H. (1957) *Games and Decisions*, John Wiley, New York.

McKenna, C. J. (1985) *Uncertainty and the Labour Market*, Wheatsheaf, Brighton.

Moore, P. G. and Thomas, H. (1976) *The Anatomy of Decisions*, Penguin, Harmondsworth.

Moore, P. G. *et al.* (1976) *Case Studies in Decision Analysis*, Penguin, Harmondsworth.

von Neumann, J. and Morgenstern, O. (1944) *Theory of Games and Economic Behaviour*, Princeton University Press, Princeton.

Newbery, D. G. M. and Stiglitz, J. E. (1981) *The Theory of Commodity Price Stabilization*, Oxford University Press, Oxford.

Pauly, M. V. (1974) 'Overinsurance and the public provision of insurance: the roles of moral hazard and adverse selection',

Quarterly Journal of Economics, **88**, 44–54. Also in Diamond and Rothschild (1978).

Pratt, J. W. (1964) 'Risk aversion in the small and in the large', *Econometrica*, **32** (1–2), January–April, 122–36. Also in Diamond and Rothschild (1978).

Rothschild, M. and Stiglitz, J. (1976) 'Equilibrium in competitive insurance markets: an essay on the economics of imperfect information', *Quarterly Journal of Economics*, **90**(4), November, 629–49. Also in Diamond and Rothschild (1978).

Savage, L. J. (1954) *The Foundations of Statistics*, John Wiley, New York.

Simon, H. A. (1959) 'Theories of decision-making in economics and behavioural science', *American Economic Review*, **49**(1), 253–83.

Spence, M. (1973) 'Job market signalling', *Quarterly Journal of Economics*, **87**, August, 355–74. Also in Diamond and Rothschild (1978).

Spence, M. and Zeckhauser, R. (1971) 'Insurance, information, and individual action', *American Economic Review* (Papers and Proceedings), **61**(2), May, 380–7. Also in Diamond and Rothschild (1978).

Stiglitz, J. E. (1983) 'Futures markets and risk: a general equilibrium approach', in Streit (1983).

Streit, M. E. (ed.) (1983) *Futures Markets: Modelling, Managing and Monitoring Futures Trading*, Blackwell, Oxford.

Tobin, J. (1958) 'Liquidity preference as behaviour towards risk', *Review of Economic Studies*, **25**, February, 65–86.

Varian, H. (1978) *Microeconomic Theory*, Norton, New York.

Index